# A CRITICAL REVIEW OF SELECTED LITERATURE ON COLLEGE STUDENT UNREST IN THE UNITED STATES, 1968-1970

# A CRITICAL REVIEW OF SELECTED LITERATURE ON COLLEGE STUDENT UNREST IN THE UNITED STATES, 1968-1970

Louis A. Foleno

Mellen Research University Press
San Francisco

**Library of Congress Cataloging-in-Publication Data**

Foleno, Louis A.
   A critical review of selected literature on college student unrest in the United States, 1968-1970 / Louis A. Foleno.
     p.   cm.
   Includes bibliographical references.
   ISBN 0-7734-9945-8
   1. Student movements--United States--History--20th century.
2. College students--United States--Political activity-
-History--20th century.   I. Title.
LA229.F55     1992
378.1'981--dc20                                        92-36849
                                                                CIP


Copyright    © 1992  Louis A. Foleno.


Editorial Inquiries:

Mellen Research University Press
534 Pacific Avenue
San Francisco
CA  94133


Order Fulfillment:

The Edwin Mellen Press
P.O. Box 450
Lewiston, NY  14092
USA


                        Printed in the United States of America

To my late Father
and
My oldest Son
Both named Anthony
and
Both Blessings

And to my youngest son, Joseph. His moral support and interest (usually at 3.00 A.M.) was indeed an incentive.

And to the "rational man" described in the Preface.

# CONTENTS

|  | Page |
|---|---|
| TABLES | ix |
| AUTHOR'S FOREWORD | xi |
| PREFACE | xiii |
| ACKNOWLEDGEMENTS | xv |
| **I. INTRODUCTION** | 1 |
| The Problem | 1 |
| The Relation of the Problem to Existing Knowledge | 3 |
| The Purpose of the Study | 12 |
| The Need and Rationale of the Study | 12 |
| Summary | 13 |
| **II. METHODOLOGICAL APPROACHES** | 15 |
| The Sociology of Knowledge | 15 |
| Delimitations of the Study | 18 |
| Definitions of Terms | 19 |
| Research Procedure and Design | 21 |
| Summary | 22 |
| **III. AN ANALYSIS OF THE SELECTED LITERATURE** | 23 |
| Overview | 23 |
| Institutional Causes | 24 |

*Contents*

| | |
|---|---|
| Socialization Causes | 49 |
| Societal Causes | 59 |
| Summary | 78 |
| **IV. SUMMARY, INTERPRETATION, AND CONCLUSION** | 83 |
| Summary | 83 |
| Interpretation | 85 |
| Conclusion | 87 |
| **V. IMPLICATIONS FOR FURTHER RESEARCH** | 91 |
| **BIBLIOGRAPHY** | 93 |

# TABLES

| | *Page* |
|---|---|
| 1. Educational Statistics on Student Enrollment and Number of Institutions of Higher Learning, 1967–70 | 3 |
| 2. Institutions Discussed in Chapter III by Four or More Authors | 80 |
| 3. Institutions Selected by the Authors Reviewed in Chapter III | 85 |
| 4. Summary of Analyses of Authors Used in the Review of Selected Literature, Chapter III | 86 |
| 5. Categories of Causes of Student Unrest from Selected Literature Authors and Author Type | 88 |
| 6. Institutions That Pertained to Three or More Authors of Selected Literature and Categories of Causes and Author Type | 89 |
| 7. Institutions Discussed by Authors of Selected Literature and Categories of Causes and Author Type | 89 |

Commendatory Foreword

One of the deficits in recent research dealing with the student unrest in the United-States from 1968 to 1970, was, until the publication of this work, the lack of critical review of the literature of the times and of the authors's own social positions and perspectives. In addition, there had been no in-depth examination of the reportage using selected literature as the sole basis for theoretical review.

Dr. Foleno has made an exhausitive study of authors who published in book form and as close to the event as possible. The great examples of the times (Berkeley, Chicago, Columbia, etc) as well as written accounts or polemics dealing with smaller settings and more local issues (such as race in the South) are discussed.

With a solid underpinning of theory drawn from the sociology of knowledge, this work has theoretical armatures that allow a general review of the literature in a most satisfactory and illuminating way. The use of the literature as the exclusive basis for interpretation interested me as an historian especially since its purpose was to find an association (if one existed) between the authors's background and their view of the causes. This same methodology was used to induce general categories of causes.

Very interestingly, the findings of Dr. Foleno's work point to the transcendance of institutional and societal causes as opposed to any authorial orientation. Often, authors who fit into liberal or progressive traditions viewed student unrest with the relish of missionaries dining with cannibals; obversely, writers who can be described as conservative or traditional observed the troubles of the time with great sympathy towards the frustration at ham-fisted bureaucracies, defense research, and military intervention in Vietnam.

As a technique or a model study, this work stands out as a welcome, distinguished contribution to sociology and, specifically, the literature of the theory of knowledge. It represents research of a high quality into the rich, perplexing literature of the day: a record that still fascinates and illuminates our own times.

Dr. Robert West<br>
San Francisco

# AUTHOR'S FOREWORD

Another Time, The Same Places

On November 27, 1963, President Lyndon B. Johnson addressed Congress, lamenting, "All I have I would have given gladly not to be standing here today." (Public papers, 1965)

These words recall John F. Kennedy's assassination. They also introduced me to the sixties.

Johnson then touched upon Vietnam, Civil Rights and the need for legislative and executive branches to act cooperatively—topics still having impact.

And now, all I have written I would gladly change if I could write about intellectual cohesiveness rather than student unrest. The turbulence of academia in the present as well as the sixties makes this study significant.

Yet, activism is not new. For 200 years students had control of medieval universities in Bologna and Padua. They did so by protests and with: "a student guild powerful enough to exact the obedience of the doctors and its members." (Cobban, 1985)

At the same time the students were not aware of the idea of a university as a social microcosm. (Cobban, 1971)

In the late 1960's protests could be seen as a result of the convergence of the Vietnam War, Civil Rights and the growth of universities. (Wallerstein, 1970)

In the 1990's we are not seeing a return to Bologna. And the 1990's are not a throwback to the 1960's. Student unrest thus far has not been similar to the past. There

*Author's Foreword*

is no focus on the institution exclusive of the society. There is no united focus on international or national issues converging.

The university of the 1990's is a microsm of United States' society. As such the issues (e.g. crime, rape, racism, freedom of expression) have divided academia as they have divided America. There is as much students against students as students against "the establishment."

The method used in my dissertation studies student unrest in a unique way, i.e. considering paradigms of causes from author's selected literature. The method of delineation offers an original starting point for a perspective that will grow with further study. In addition, this method may be used to study student unrest in 1991, 1400, 1968, etc. Careful examination could provide a valuable analysis since both sides may see and research only their role.

> Thus, "The liberal observer saw the student activist as enlightened, able, idealistic. The conservative saw him as frivolous, undisciplined, self-righteous. Each could find data to support his own view." (pp. ix–x)
>
> Roger W. Heyns in Foreword to Keplemen (1972)

I am honored to have this study considered to be a "Distinguished Dissertation." The format and content of a dissertation, as well as its audience, dictates a definite style. My future studies will have another style but the same spirit. Hopefully the reader will obtain historical insight and a procedure to examine literature on student unrest.

A love of academia, teaching and research and a desire to continue to write on higher education are cherished dividends of this study. I have also been fortunate from my "socialization" as a student at the University of Scranton and Rutgers Graduate School of Education, and having learned from my students and colleagues at City University of New York, The College of Staten Island.

# PREFACE

However, it is not enough merely to be exposed to diverse sources of information. A rational man can perceive without distortion and remember accurately even information which radically disagrees with his own opinions or runs counter to his thinking. He does not simply attend to those arguments which are consonant with his beliefs, nor remember that which bolsters his prejudices. In short, to be rational a man must expose himself to congenial and uncongenial matters alike. He must be able to look at both and perceive them as they are, not merely as he would like them to be, and he must be able to retain this information in undistorted form. (p. 74)

*Robert E. Lane*
*and*
*David O. Sears*
*1964*

# ACKNOWLEDGEMENTS

Dr. Donald Halsted, Department of Social and Philosophical Foundations of Education, Rutgers University, was the teacher who first challenged and encouraged my interest in research and in the sociology of education. Dr. James E. Wheeler, Dr. Joseph James Chamblisss, Dr. Adam Scrupski, Dr. William M. Phillips, Jr., and Dr. Hal Graham Lewis offered encouragement and manifested interest with timely advice. All reflected the academic spirit and talent found in the Rutgers Department of Social and Philosophical Foundations of Education.

Dr. Mariagnes Lattimer offered her time and procedural expertise. This resulted in the Scholarship Committee granting me the Charles Sumner Crow Scholarship, which enabled me to continue my research.

The Reference Department of Rutgers University Alexander Library provided effective, efficient, and humane assistance — especially Mr. Seymour Swerdling and Mrs. Hedwig Seitz.

Mr. Philip Hughes, Ph.D. candidate in Sociology, Rutgers, had offered valuable methodological suggestions.

Mr. Robert Walton, Director of the Prison Education Network; Dean Donald Suppers; and Dr. Sabra Meservey, all of Mercer College, gave me their perceptions on student unrest.

Dr. Simon Marcson, Sociology Department, Rutgers, gave me a valuable opportunity to research institutions from an organizational perspective.

Dr. Luciano Rusich and Mr. David Levine are both teachers and friends. Their candid suggestions made revisions easier, and they kept me on target.

## Acknowledgements

My students and the authors with whom I corresponded on student unrest and sociology of knowledge are too numerous to mention. However, their encouragement, confidence, and research referrals and suggestions have permeated my writings.

Members of my dissertation committee, Dr. Donald Lyle Halsted, Dr. Nobuo Shimahara, Dr. Kenneth Donald Carlson, and Dr. Bernard Goldstein, were insistent regarding procedure and content in the proposal and dissertation. Their analytical questions and knowledge of this topic from different perspectives helped to refine and define both methodology and content.

Dr. Nobuo Shimahara, Chairman of the Social and Philosophical Foundations of Education Department, had been my most demanding teacher and also the most encouraging. My first paper on student unrest was for one of his courses.

My father-in-law, Rudolph Drexler, provided guidelines and resource persons in translating German vocabulary on sociology of knowledge concepts.

Dr. Arthur Spangenberg provided impressive analytical and design suggestions.

My wife, Barbara, was in the most beautiful sense my most reliable critic. She was also understanding, patient, and supportive beyond expectation.

# I
# INTRODUCTION

Student unrest throughout the world and, most relevant to this study, in the United States of America was a social phenomenon of note. This was an existent phenomenon from 1964 to 1970 which showed an increase in both volume and violence from 1968 to 1970 on college campuses across the United States.

## THE PROBLEM

During the 1968 to 1970 period college student unrest was not construed as an isolated incident or even as a series of isolated incidents. Neither was it to be credited to a few students at a few four-year institutions of higher learning.

While many factors were examined in the abundant body of literature which recorded and commented upon student unrest, no overall scheme of analysis was consistently utilized. Inquiries into the basic question (why particular groups of students, faculty, and supportive association of men and women, at a particular point in time, at particular place—the college—do participate in a particular form of radical action) have yet to arrive at an analysis that is consistent or broadly acceptable. There were no arguments about the de facto existence of student unrest, but differences regarding perceptions of issues and causes have yet to be resolved. An analogous situation would be a fist fight between two students witnessed by others present in the classroom from diverse vantage points of observation and interest. Although both the participants and witnesses would agree that the fist fight occurred, their analyses could differ regarding the issues and causes.

*Introduction* 2

John P. Spiegel (1973), in his paper, *Campus Disorders: A Transactional Approach*, written for the Lemberg Center for the Study of Violence contended that:

> In all the varied comment on campus disorders little attention has been paid to the group process and the dynamic interactions that create the various factions, on and off campus, and set them into such intransigent, antagonistic and occasionally violent relations with each other. (p. 473)

Based upon his observations of student unrest Spiegel was impressed with the effect of these group processes and dynamic interactions. His analysis of inconsistencies in what is remembered and what is forgotten follows:

> There are two related aspects of the aftermath. . . . The first is "the Rashomon effect," the varying and often incompatible stories that are told of what transpired during the crisis. Interviewers from the media and committees appointed to review the events are frequently surprised by the conflicting narrations of supposedly the same incident obtained from different persons. Certainly this is not a new finding in the history of psychology. The surprise occurs because the discrepancies are so blatant and the witnesses so credible. The second matter has to do not with inconsistencies in what people remember, but with what they "forget." To be sure, with so much happening from hour to hour, no one can witness much less recall the whole spectrum of events. What stands out, however, is the inability of people to remember things that they themselves have said and done, although others can retain it vividly. (p. 486)

Also, the literature, for example, as referred to in the bibliographies of Altbach (1968), Aptheker (1973), Dunlop (1969), Segal (1960), and Altbach and Kelly (1973), reflected similar inconsistencies to those mentioned above as well as other diverse studies and methodologies of inquiry on the nature of student unrest.

This problem of inconsistency suggested that it might be valuable to examine the explanatory framework used by selected writers. The major thrust of this study would be to select a body of literature and examine the explanations given by the writers. Theoretical considerations suggest that the explanations given may be, in part, either a bias of the writer or relatively independent of such bias.

In summary, many hypotheses were advanced regarding the evolution and causes of student unrest. There was, however, no consistent overall scheme used to examine authors' perceptions of causes as they are found solely in the literature. Hence, the central problem of this study was to critically examine some of the explanations given to specific instances of student unrest.

## THE RELATION OF THE PROBLEM TO EXISTING KNOWLEDGE

This study will concentrate, for methodological reasons, on literature selected according to specific criteria. In all cases these studies deal with incidents on specific campuses across the United States. This selection should not suggest that there were not other concerns over what appeared to be a national phenomenon.

In keeping with the spirit of this inquiry, it would seem appropriate to establish the dimensions of this phenomenon. Obviously there was something occurring which made incidents the target of inquiry by these and other authors.

The material in this section offers an overview of such incidents. Table 1 gives an indication of the total number of students and institutions that were potential subjects or targets of study regarding student unrest.

The U.S. Congress Senate (1969), *Staff Study of Campus Riots and Disorders, October 1967-May 1969*, offered a statistical summary of campus disturbances covering the period of October 1967 to May 1969. It reported 471 disturbances involving 211 colleges. There were approximately 598 injuries according to the staff study estimates.

A survey of 40,000 students conducted by the National Student Association in *The Chronicle of Higher Education,* "101 Campuses Identified as Demonstration Scenes"

TABLE 1
EDUCATIONAL STATISTICS ON STUDENT ENROLLMENT AND NUMBER OF INSTITUTIONS OF HIGHER LEARNING, 1967–1970

| Year | Student Enrollment | Institutions of Higher Learning |
|---|---|---|
| 1967[a] | 6,911,748 | 2,374 |
| 1968[b] | 7,513,901 | 2,483 |
| 1969[c] | 7,916,991 | 2,525 |
| 1970[d] | 8,498,117 | 2,556 |

[a] K. A. Simon and W. V. Grant (Eds.), *Digest of Educational Statistics*, 1968 edition (Washington, D.C.: Government Printing Office, 1969), pp. 83, 64.
[b] Ibid., 1969 edition, pp. 68, 60.
[c] Ibid., 1970 edition, pp. 85, 62
[d] Ibid., 1971 edition, pp. 83, 66.

(September 2, 1968, p. 5) indicated that 221 demonstrations occurred at 101 colleges during the latter half of the 1967–1968 school year. These demonstrations involved 38,900 students.

In a study for the American Council on Education Office of Research, Bayer and Astin (1969) reported that in the school year of 1968–1969 approximately 145

(6.2%) of the 2,300 colleges and universities had at least one incident of violent protest. An additional estimated 379 or 16.2% of the colleges and universities experienced non-violent but disruptive protest. The initial sample for these estimates contained 427 colleges and universities (79 of which were two-year colleges).

The Urban Research Corporation (1970) reported 292 major student protests which occurred on 232 college and university campuses in the first six months of 1969.

J. Edgar Hoover, then director of the Federal Bureau of Investigation, reported over 4,000 arrests during the 1968–1969 school year stemming from disruptive and violent protests and approximately 7,200 similar arrests during 1969–1970 (*U.S. News and World Report*, May 18, 1970, pp. 28–31).

*The Report of the President's Commission on Campus Unrest* (1970) is quoted at length regarding student unrest in May 1970:

> On April 30, 1970, President Nixon announced that American and South Vietnamese forces were moving against enemy sanctuaries in Cambodia. Minutes after this announcement, student-organized protest demonstrations were under way at Princeton and Oberlin College. Within a few days, strikes and other protests had taken place at scores of colleges and universities throughout the country.
>
> The expanding wave of strikes brought with it some serious disturbances. One of these was at Kent State University in Ohio, and approximately 750 Ohio National Guardsmen were sent to quell the disorders there.
>
> On May 2, the ROTC building at Kent State was set afire. On May 4, Kent State students congregated on the University Commons and defied an order by the Guard to disperse. Guardsmen proceeded to disperse the crowd. The students then began to taunt Guard units and to throw rocks. The Guardsmen fired tear gas into the crowd, and then some fired their weapons. Four students were killed, and nine were wounded.
>
> During the six days after the President's announcement of the Cambodian incursion, but prior to the deaths at Kent State, some twenty new student strikes had begun each day. During the four days that followed the Kent killings, there were a hundred or more strikes each day. A student strike center located at Brandeis University reported that, by the 19th of May, 448 campuses were either still affected by some sort of strike or completely closed down.
>
> Ten days after the events at Kent State there were disturbances at Jackson State College, a black school in Jackson, Mississippi. On the night of May 14, students threw bricks and bottles at passing white motorists, a truck was set ablaze, and city and state police, called to protect firemen, were harassed by the crowd. Two blacks were killed, and at least twelve were wounded.

> Other schools joined the student strike, and many temporarily suspended classes in memory of those killed at Jackson State. By the end of May, according to statistics compiled by the Urban Research Corporation, nearly one-third of the approximately 2,500 colleges and universities in America had experienced some kind of protest activity. The high point of the strikes were during the week following the deaths at Kent State. (pp. 17–18)

Peterson and Bilorusky (1971) offered an overview of the campus reactions to Cambodia, Kent State, and Jackson State. Fifty-seven percent of the nation's colleges (approximately 1,350) experienced "significant impact." Seventy-seven percent of these were peaceful.

An article by Carleton (1969) claimed that a small minority was involved in student activism. Horowitz and Friedland (1972) and Keniston (1971) claimed not only that the percentage of students involved in student unrest was small, but that the number of affected campuses, despite increases, was also small.

Yet, Horowitz and Friedland (1972) also reflected:

> The dominant inertness, however, should not be allowed to detract from the social significance of student demonstrations. All revolutions are initiated by small numbers of people, and even at the peak of revolutionary action the bulk of the population is *not* involved. (p. 7)

It will be noted by the reader that in all these studies different sources and types of facts were utilized. No specific aggregate of data was taken to be more valid than another. Regardless of the data used, what emerges clearly is that the United States college students were involved in a type of activity on the campuses which was neither usual nor to be ignored.

Foster and Long (1970) edited an anthology on the student protest movement. Of particular interest was Foster's (Foster & Long, 1970) article on varied orientations of liberals and radicals. The article also provided a bibliography on student protest with an emphasis on the period of 1965–1970. Foster and Long (1970) presented five sections of readings with their introductory comments on I. The Conflict (overviews), II. The Activists (personal background), III. Scenes of Conflict (seven case studies), IV. New Patterns of Power (generalizations), and V. Perspectives on Protest (interpretations). They maintained that observer objectivity was difficult to ensure in that the great number of activities that took place concurrently necessitated selectivity of facts presented (pp. 226–228).

Ellsworth and Burns (1970) treated student unrest descriptively, historically, and analytically. Their work included an extensive selected bibliography of philosophical, psychological, and empirical studies regarding the phenomenon. However, this work did not concern itself with any study of the literature similar to that proposed by the writer. Descriptions of current unrest reflected no consistent method of observation and were limited to particular institutions and points in time. The historical treatment of student unrest in the United States cited data on past events which could be compared to or contrasted with current trends. The analytical portion of the work offered causative factors relating to the personality of the student, the type of institution, and general causes found in areas outside the institution and the individual. The authors proposed that the current unrest had developed from the sit-ins of the early 1960s by students who were actively seeking to desegregate the southern institutions. Also, considerable attention was focused upon the psychological profiles of the early CORE and SNICK activists and how the frustration and disillusionments they experienced influenced later activists to employ confrontation tactics.

Wrong (1972) commented on the state of that year's literature in a book-review essay. He maintained that publication of such a quantity of analyses in close proximity of time to the actual events had serious implications for the nature of scholarly studies:

> It is doubtful that any other events in American history have been submitted to such instantaneous and intensive analysis by as many *experts writing from such a wide variety of perspectives* [emphasis added]. The usual time lag between the initial publication of journalistic quickies and firsthand accounts by participants, and the later appearance of scholarly studies by social scientists, has been abbreviated almost to the vanishing point. (p. 66)

Keniston (1973) made a comprehensive and noteworthy contribution to the topic in his bibliography of 303 empirical studies regarding student activism, radicalism, and institutions where protests occurred. He located and abstracted the research since World War II and offered an introduction which examined the hypotheses. He concluded:

> These abstracts should make clear that anyone seeking clear answers, expecting neat comparability between studies conducted at different colleges, convinced of the inevitably "progressive" nature of social science, or unwilling to make distinctions, will be acutely frustrated by the literature. (p. xv)

Keniston (1973) also notes:

> In much of the research reviewed, the level of methodological and theoretical sophistication is not very high. Taking the literature as a whole, it is notable

how rarely elementary distinctions have been made and to the detriment of the results. (p. ix)

Keniston's analysis of two theories led him to conclude that intergenerational continuity and intergenerational conflict theories are not necessarily opposite, and that the same kind of data may support both points of view (p. ix). The intergenerational conflict theory maintained that the students were rebelling against middle-class and authoritarian concepts they perceived in their parents' generation. The gap between youth and parents was attributed to a dissatisfaction with middle-class values and life styles. The intergenerational continuity theory maintained that students were simply putting into practice those values that their parents had only preached.

Keniston (1973) found both theories could be compatible if students were considered rebelling—not against middle-class authority—but against a social system they found to be hypocritical, a system that taught them to question and to act upon their beliefs only when such actions did not upset the status quo. The revolt was both in conflict and in a continuum with the preceding generation. It was against a system which had taught them one standard but opposed their logical implementation of this standard. Within this system, the students were in agreement with parents who, according to youth's criterion, continued to implement this standard.

In a study of student protest movements in the United States and Europe during the 19th and 20th centuries, Feuer (1969) gave a psychological explanation of the young and their revolt against the established (by their parents) authority. Student radicals were considered by Feuer to be conducting, in his analysis, an intergenerational struggle that had been ongoing throughout history. His bibliography was an extensive compilation of historical and psychological studies relating to student protest.

Horowitz and Friedland (1972) cited three general theories they found in the literature. They are: (a) conspiracy theory, (b) social-structural theories, and (c) student-cultural changes. The authors maintained, however, that these were only underlying factors, and placed greater emphasis on the convergence of the Black Revolution and the Vietnam War as chief causes and issues. In yet another anthology, Whiteley (1970) offered a broad spectrum of readings ranging from social-activists factors to the intergenerational-conflict theory. Hypotheses, referrals to statistical research, chronologies, and demographic studies were found in Peterson and Bilorusky (1971). The President's Commission on Campus Unrest (*The Report of the President's Commission on Campus Unrest*, 1970) offered a concise summary of causes and an extensive annotated bibliography, while the Carnegie Commission (1971) gave a summary of recommendations of their committee as well as other investigative commissions.

As a result of his research, Searle (1971) listed 11 underlying causes of student unrest. It should be noted that a further general analysis of this list resulted in the establishment of two categories: causes external to the universities and causes internal or endemic to the universities. Searle defined external causes as those having origins in factors outside institutions of higher learning. One such cause noted was the affluence of students which enabled them to give more time to expressing their concerns or to assuaging guilt feelings about those less fortunate than themselves (hence their involvement in Civil Rights and the Vietnam War). Another external factor lay in child-rearing styles which resulted in students being highly impatient with impersonal bureaucracy and also oriented them to question and resist any system perceived as unjustly elitist or ineffectual. Another external cause noted was the students' perception of the institutions in our society as obsolete and really unresponsive to current social needs. An example of such an institution could be one of the federal government bureaucracies. Finally, Searle mentioned the crises of authority and discussed the problem of the generation gap. The students experienced a loss of respect for authority and authority figures which they perceived as bureaucratic, impersonal, and hypocritical.

The seven internal causes that Searle outlined were related to the external causes mentioned above. For example, there arose a crisis in education philosophy over the issue of relevance. The students and colleges were in marked disagreement as to what should be taught and why. Also considered was the role of media and the sheer numbers of incidents that were given "prime time." Searle maintained that the extensive media coverage created a climate conducive to more incidents. Similar to their perceptions of institutions in general, students viewed the university structure as irrelevant to their social and academic needs and concerns. Furthermore, students also had a prolonged period of dependency on adults and they deplored the "service station"—impersonal university. Searle also noted that in their unrest students were reacting against technology because they feared that rapid change would render them more helpless or alienated. Finally, Searle saw, at the least, a simplistic imitation (based in part on any of the above cases) of other protestors.

In *The Academy in Turmoil* (1970), the authors contended that unrest evolved from sources of the Civil Rights Movement, a subculture and the general context of national-international problems. Up to February 1, 1970, it was cited that the San

Francisco State events in the spring of 1968 were seen as the most notorious example of student unrest. The work offered case studies and an analysis of student unrest in New York colleges and universities.

Wallerstein (1970) viewed the phenomenon of United States college student unrest (1965-1970) as a consequence of three convergent strains: (a) the Vietnam War, (b) the role of blacks in the United States society, and (c) the growth in size of the universities. Harold Taylor (1970) expanded this line of reasoning and viewed student activities in the United States as part of a world student movement. Significant commonalities among students of various nations were mentioned by Taylor:

> On the whole, they are anti-bureaucratic, anti-war and are critical of the structure and content of university education in a wide range of objections, from the examination system and the admissions programs to the role of students in the decision-making connected with the university policy and government. (p. 40)

Toole (1970) saw student unrest as the actions of spoiled children and was highly critical and unsympathetic to their methods. Bloomberg (1970) condemned violent demonstration as a kind of unreasoning anti-intellectualism. In addition, he blamed permissive faculties and administrations for abdicating their responsibilities in the face of student demonstrations and criticized institutions which negotiated under the ground rules of pressure and violence. A different opinion was expressed by Flacks (1970) in a review and interpretation of empirical studies of student protestors. Student unrest, according to Flacks (1970), was caused by the reactions of students of a certain social background against social-structural and institutional situations. These reactions were due in part to the students' moral commitment to humanistic values. Flacks (1970) also noted the influence of secondary socialization by activist groups which many students empathized with or joined. According to Peterson and Bilorusky (1971) the early studies by Flacks, Katz, and Keniston presented student activists as being brighter than their conservative counterparts. Yet Kepelman, Watts, and Whittaker found that these students were not brighter but simply more prone to act on principles in which they believed (Peterson & Bilorusky, 1971, pp. 94–96).

Research indicated that brightness, not necessarily reflected in grades, was a common trait of college activist students—especially at highly selective colleges and regardless of ideology. According to Peterson and Bilorusky (1971), the critical mass phenomenon and the general student body were factors that seemed more important than intelligence, intergenerational conflict, or intergenerational agreement (p. 41).

The social exchange theory, according to Kornstein and Weissenberg (1970), assumes that students and institutions could exchange something that would be of mutual benefit. However, the students could offer nothing more than a promise to end violence or disruption, and these authors maintained that such a commodity should not be equal to what the institutions could offer. This arrangement was considered to be blackmail rather than sound collateral for student demands, and the authors found the social exchange theory impractical as a general theory to explain the phenomenon of unrest (pp. 447–456).

Lipset (1971) provided a historical analysis of the evolution of the protest movement from the early 60s to 1970. He outlined sources of student activism (Chapter I), provided statistical studies (Chapter II), and gave psychological and sociological profiles of the activists (Chapter III). Lipset's emphasis was on structural factors of the institution and the types of students prone to activist behavior. He reported that in view of the SDS, the establishment ideology was created to justify the existence of dominant social groups.

According to Stevenson (1972), the SDS had adopted the "sociology of knowledge" as an approach to social problems. This approach offered the possibility for "viewing social concerns from a radically different perspective" (p. 87). For example:

> Oglesby sought, quite specifically to convey this distinction to SDSers in order to expose what he saw as distortions in liberal thinking. His 1965 Washington speech on Vietnam, entitled "Trapped by the System," admonished his listeners to throw away the habit of thinking that a very bad war (Vietnam) must be caused by very bad men.
> (Stevenson, 1972, P. 89)

Interrelated and convergent factors, such as institutional and racial, were discussed by Stevenson within the context of the type of students involved in activism due to these factors and the predispositions of these students.

Stevenson (1972) also presented a review of literature on activists in his introduction and gave emphasis to the activist role of the Students for a Democratic Society. His review was a summary of works relating to political activists. He divided the literature into three areas: (a) empirical studies by sociologists and psychologists, (b) critical and interpretative commentary by nonmovement academic and journalist authors, and (c) analyses by authors associated with the activist movement.

Stevenson's comments on the SDS as an activist movement were indeed an important segment of his study. His review of the literature, footnote commentaries, bibliography, and appendix contained references on the literature sources and chronology of student activists' activities from 1960 to 1968. Of special importance are his references to contemporary anthologies and SDS literature. Studies by several authors pointed to the SDS as a catalyst for student unrest. Similar to Stevenson's analysis, Wallerstein and Starr's *The University Crisis Reader*, Vols. 1 and 2 (1971), had as its theme the radical attack on the liberal university and resultant confrontation and counterattack by the university. The editors collected, organized, and offered introductory and running comments upon primary literature appearing on both sides of the conflict, 1965–1970, with emphasis on the later years. Primary sources authorized by those in the radical student movement and also an appendix of "student demands." were additional contributions to the research related to student unrest.

Halleck (1972) categorized 12 hypotheses of student unrest into three groups: (a) critical, (b) sympathetic, and (c) neutral. He believed that the neutral hypotheses were the most intriguing and valid explanations of student unrest.

The critical hypotheses categorized unrest as "temper tantrums" of students who resorted to violating the rights of others to effect what they perceived as necessary changes in life style, values, and institutions. Hypotheses were categorized as sympathetic if they viewed students as having legitimate complaints against society and its institutions. The neutral hypotheses proposed that both the purpose and methods of the activists should be examined in each particular case. Neutral authors maintained that the style and substance of student unrest were too complex to allow either for the condonation or condemnation of student unrest as a general movement.

> The causes of unrest according to these hypotheses are not to be found in the actions or philosophies of other men, but are believed to reside in changes in our highly complex society which seem to create the need for new modes of psychological adaptation. (Halleck, 1972, p. 97)

Although numerous, the preceding comments on the existence of student unrest and the types of explanations offered were not exhaustive. In view of the voluminous literature, an inclusion or simple citation of all the studies thus far discovered by this writer would have made this section excessively encyclopedic. The literature was copious, and it was enough to have offered indications of its magnitude and nature. This writer's intention was to provide examples of its quantity and the numerous kinds of research and explanations that have been thus far advanced.

## The Purpose of the Study

The purpose of the study was to examine how selected authors explained student unrest. One way of concentrating on this purpose was to review and analyze the selected literature based upon considerations obtained from the sociology of knowledge. This perspective (sociology of knowledge) suggests that the interpretation of events may not stem directly from characteristics inherent in the event so much as the interaction of the event and the characteristics of the observer. This study then, attempts a critical analysis of the interpretations of student unrest concentrating on both the "facts" as reported by the author and the role of the author in the event. What this study then attempts is similar to Robert Merton's (1968) comments about a paradigm. Merton stated that a paradigm "does not represent a set of categories introduced *de novo* but rather a codification of those concepts and problems which have been forced upon our attention by critical scrutiny of current research and theory" (p. 104).

The organization of this study was to: (a) select a certain body of significant literature; (b) review and analyze this literature to ascertain how the authors explained student unrest; (c) examine these explanations and also information about the authors as induced solely from the literature; and (d) determine if the authors' experiences and orientations pertaining to student unrest were reflected in their explanations.

## The Need and Rationale of the Study

> The earthly issues and tactics of protest engendered problems by 1970 that virtually no one in 1964 had predicted. The first issues were occupation of physical space, varieties of rudeness, ingenious harassment. But the tactics escalated to armed confrontation (Cornell), mob violence (Berkeley), arson (Stanford), blackmail (San Francisco State), and murder (Wisconsin). We became accustomed to the destruction of records and property and the disruption of education. (Berman, 1974, p. 14)

The social phenomenon of student unrest during 1968 to 1970 may also have implications for the future. Halleck (1972), in his analysis of the hypotheses advanced on student unrest, maintained that "a determined minority of restless college students has forced us to examine and sometimes change institutions, rules and values which were once considered inviolate" (p. 89). Bakke and Bakke (1971), writing about international student rebellion, stated in *Campus Challenge* that "student activism must be taken seriously" (p. 6). They also claimed that potential impact on both colleges and public policy was noteworthy (p. 6).

Student unrest in colleges and universities was a decidedly significant phenomenon that affected a large number of institutions and a large number of people. There has been no review of the literature as proposed by this writer and so the thrust of this analysis has been to examine how such a sociological phenomenon was explained by a selected segment of the explainers. Accordingly, a limited number of works were reviewed and analyzed in an endeavor to see if the explanations offered tell us more about the explainer than they do about the actual phenomenon. In other words, the purpose of this study is to provide insight into *how* student unrest was explained rather than an analysis of the movement itself.

Since this study concerned itself with what was being said rather than the actual event, a decision was made to use the selected literature as an exclusive source. The purpose was to discover what can be learned and induced from such an analysis of limited data and to determine what value this analysis would have as a foundation for further study.

## SUMMARY

In this chapter, evidence has been presented on the existence of student unrest as a social phenomenon. The time (1968–1970) and place (United States colleges) were established as the objects of inquiry. An overview of various types of studies published on student unrest gave no indication that any study to date had reviewed the literature for the purpose of examining the explanations solely from the perspective of the selected literature. Such an examination would focus more upon what was said about the phenomenon rather than upon the phenomenon itself. The nature of the impact of student unrest and present state of the research were two reasons given to establish the need and rationale for this study.

# II
# METHODOLOGICAL APPROACHES

### The Sociology of Knowledge

The causes of student unrest had been thus far studied in two different manners. Some authors offered in-depth studies of particular colleges, while others sought to formulate general causal hypotheses. In this study, the literature was analyzed according to what the authors said and what their particular frames of reference were; for a frame of reference may "profoundly influence one's observations, interpretations, and judgments in a social situation" (Theodorson & Theodorson, 1969, p. 61). This method of analysis could prove effective in this study, especially with relation to what has been done previously: "Numerous causal hypotheses have been advanced but few attempts have been made at developing a conceptual framework within which protest can be understood" (Kornstein & Weissenberg, 1970, p. 447). What was lacking was a model for examination of what had been said, when it was said, and who said it; hence, the consideration, research, and evolution of the proposed methodology.

In looking at the literature on the sociology of knowledge it appeared that this literature might provide insights helpful to develop a method for this inquiry.

Some conceptual frameworks and definitions were derived from a review of the works of Bart and Frankel (1971), Berger (1963), Berger and Berger (1972), Berger and Luckman (1967), Curtis and Petras (1972), Robert Merton (1968), and Stark (1967). Curtis and Petras (1972) viewed the sociology of knowlegde as a fairly

## Chapter II

inconsistent frame of reference used by sociologists rather than a definite body of theory in its own right, and they did point to the near impossibility of defining sociology of knowledge (pp.1, 7). Similarly, Berger and Luckman (1967) commented upon the vague status of a definition and also referred to certain commonalities:

> There have been *different definitions* of the nature and scope of the sociology of knowledge. Indeed, it might almost be said that the history of the subdiscipline thus far has been the history of its various definitions. Nevertheless, there has been *general agreement* to the effect that the sociology of knowledge is concerned with the relationship between *human thought and the social context within which it arises* [emphasis added]. (p. 4)

The sociology of knowledge, therefore, is best viewed as a broad concept rather than a concrete theory having a basic definition as a point of departure.

Originally, with Scheler of the "European School," the mind and society were considered as equal variables. Furthermore, knowledge arose from the interaction of the historical process with these variables. According to Scheler and many theorists in Germany and France, there did exist general categories of thought which were influenced by the social order. Scheler's "real factor" was the independent variable which consisted of meanings given to ideas in light of a particular social situation. Theorists noted that the elite were able to grasp phenomenological essences and attempted to use the sociology of knowledge to distinguish such elite, essential knowledge from knowledge of the masses. These considerations lead to lone scholars analyzing book-form data. There was systematic review and appraisal of how knowledge and modes of thought were affected by the social order and particular attention was paid to the basic ideas of the elite. Such theorists of knowledge were described as marginal to social classes and thus took notice of diverse ways of perceiving reality. However, in spite of this ideological transcendence, there remained a significant problem of reliability.

Theorists vary in their analyses of these issues. Robert Merton (1968), in his analysis, perceived ideology as a rationale for those who wanted to maintain the status quo. According to his view, ideology determined what passed for knowledge. Marx considered economic ideology as the dominant force in defining knowledge while Mannheim saw the theorists working within the ideology of his social group (Merton, 1968, Chapter VI).

Durkheim and the French crowd psychologists were concerned with the influence of current society. They maintained that society produced a collective consciousness, and this was more influenced by the social milieu than by historical ideas. The collective consciousness represented a total view of the world determined by the context of a social situation. The individual's thoughts were extensions of this world view (Curtis & Petras, 1972, pp. 2–3).

In the United States, there was little focus on theory. Rather than working on bookform data, scholars conducted empirical studies. Also, there was more concern about knowledge of the masses than about the knowledge of the elite.

According to Curtis and Petras (1972):

> The frames of reference utilized by the three branches can be characterized briefly as follows. The German branch tended to combine a philosophical spiritualism with *"Verstehende Soziologie"* and a concern for the universal process for history. The French branch epitomized in the works of Durkheim and the crowd psychologists emphasized the relation between individual minds and society, as well as the structuring influence of the particular socio-cultural environment. Historical processes were deemphasized in favour of the connection between the mind of the individual and a particular time. The most prominent feature of the American tradition has been its emphasis on interdependence as the essential variable in understanding the relationship between the individual and the socio-cultural groups. (pp. 6–7)

In addition to the above, this theme was noted by Thomas Ford Hoult (1974) when he stated that the sociology of knowledge must concern itself with "the substantive and/or methodological implications of the idea that knowledge is a function of culture and social structure" (p. 308).

Hoult's comments suggest that the use of selected literature as data in this study could have such methodological implications, especially when such data would be considered knowledge for analysis. As stated by Berger and Luckman (1967) in reference to the idea of "knowledge":

> The sociology of knowledge must concern itself with whatever passes by "knowledge" in a society, regardless of the ultimate validity or invalidity (by whatever criteria) of such "knowledge." And insofar as all human "knowledge" is developed, transmitted and maintained in social situations, the sociology of knowledge must seek to understand the process by which this is done in such a way that a taken-for-granted "reality" congeals for the man in the street. (p. 3)

There is, therefore, a broad range of concepts regarding the sociology of knowledge including the knowledge of a particular situation (Hoult, 1974, p. 100), popular majority opinion and mass trend setters (Merton, 1968, pp. 493–542), common sense knowledge (Douglas, 1970, pp. 3–44), and the knowledge of laymen (Merton, 1968, pp. 496–497). Finally, there is the issue of the value of a sociology of knowledge orientation: "In its ability to separate and segregate reality from fantasy, science from ideology, the sociology of knowledge is able to avoid the capriciousness of individual genius and collective blindness alike" (Horowitz, 1968, p. 27).

While formulating a method, i.e., "specific techniques involved in a particular study" (Hoult, 1974, p. 203), this writer utilized certain conceptual commonalities that were found in the review of the sociology of knowledge.

*Wissenssoziologie* was determined to mean a study of knowledge of society, with knowledge of how certain authors wrote on student unrest as its specific object. The selected authors may have viewed the same or similar phenomenon from different perspectives. These diverse views could have been influenced by:

1. The author's background, his orientation to the phenomena or secondary socialization (*unterbau*); and

2. The author's particular experience or involvement with student unrest (*ueberbau*).

As previously stated, this writer's focus was on the authors and selected literature rather than the causes per se. The causes given by the authors of the selected literature are not mutually exclusive; they may exist on a continuum or concurrently. An attempt has been made here to analyze the selected literature and ascertain what was construed by each author to be the chief cause and how the work illuminated and elaborated upon the cause. Of course, this kind of analysis has no control over the diverse styles and content selection of the authors reviewed. Rather, it seeks to construct a framework to elucidate and examine what was written.

Fleming (1975) and Adelson (1974) are two authors who indicated concern about the quality of research that was done at a time proximate to the events of student unrest. Keniston (1973) also criticized the quality of the research of such literature. Similarly, Wrong (1972) deplored the lack of an efficient time lag and found that the proximity in time to the actual events was a hindrance to writers. It was with these issues in mind that the present analysis was undertaken.

## DELIMITATIONS OF THE STUDY

Due to voluminous literature on student unrest, certain limitations were inherent in the methodology of selection and analysis of data (i.e., a specific type of literature on United States college student unrest).

## Chapter II

The selection of data was confined to literature pertaining to a particular time and space. The time was 1968–1970. Literature published before the Columbia University unrest (April 1968), or dealing with events after the Kent State University unrest (May 1970), was not included. The space included only United States colleges or universities. Student unrest literature relating to a cross-cultural or international perspective was not included. Literature on schools other than four-year colleges was not considered. Also excluded were writings relevant to United States college student unrest 1968–1970, unpublished or not in book form, and writings in anthology or multiauthor forms.

To summarize, both the selection and the analysis of data did not go beyond the selected literature. Student unrest was examined by this writer exclusively on the basis of such information, for to do otherwise would have violated the purpose of this study. Addenda would have contaminated the method of determining what could be learned from the proposed analysis. Finally, this analysis had as its limited object how the causes of student unrest were explained. It did not concern itself with the causes per se.

### DEFINITIONS OF TERMS

The definitions were more developmental than normative.

*Author's involvement.* Throughout the study, this term pertained to the authors of the selected literature. It refers to the manner in which the authors were involved in actual events of unrest or come to be on the scene either shortly after the event or while the climate of unrest was still viable and current.

*Cause.* Throughout the study, the term "cause" included many concepts. These were conditions, catalysts, triggering factors, proximate causes, primary cause intensifications, escalations, causes of containment, social determinants, and underlying causes. Although the writer extended the term to cover these concepts, it was specifically used to delineate certain factors which according to the selected authors resulted in a particular type of student unrest. This broad definition of "cause" was necessary when confronted with the wide diversity of reasons offered for unrest in the literature.

*College.* Throughout this study, the term "college" referred to four-year colleges, universities, and graduate schools which experienced some degree of student unrest.

*Frame of reference.* Throughout this study, student unrest was perceived by selected authors in relation to something. The something was the frame of reference which served the authors as a guide for interpreting this particular phenomenon.

Two relevant definitions are:

> The frame of reference of social action theory used to analyze social and personality systems. It focuses on the actor (or actors), his values and goals, in *specific situations* [emphasis added]. (Theodorson & Theodorson, 1969, p. 6)
>
> In the social sciences, particularly in sociology, an interrelated set of ideas that served as a guide or basis for interpreting *particular phenomena* [emphasis added]. (Hoult, 1974, p. 136)

*Institutional.* Throughout this study, the term "institutional" pertained to the specific type(s) of bureaucratic/structural organizations found in colleges or universities.

*Methodological.* Throughout this study, the term "methodological" pertained to research tools, procedural factors in selection of topics and data, and to how these related to both the authors of the selected literature and the writer of this study.

*Primary socialization.* Throughout this study, the term "primary socialization" was used to encompass those experiences and attitudes closely associated with child rearing and family or peer values. Chronologically and structurally, primary socialization refers to influences much prior to those of 1968–1970; i.e., before the authors' involvement with or observations of the institutions and events of 1968–1970 that relate to student unrest.

*Professional writer (or journalist).* Throughout this study, the term "professional writer" (or journalist) referred to a person who had as his chief occupation and source of income the profession of writing. Certainly, all of the authors used in Chapter III were writers. However, some had as their chief occupation the position of student, college administrator, or faculty.

*Secondary socialization.* Throughout this study, the term "secondary socialization" was used to encompass experiences and attitudes closely associated with involvement, attendance, or pressure in college.

Chronologically, secondary socialization came after primary, but it may have been an extension of primary socialization or a refutation. This writer's focus was on the secondary socialization of the authors which took place at the institutions just prior to the time covered in this study (1968–1970), during the actual events, or shortly thereafter.

Structurally, secondary socialization related to socialization relatively concurrent with the student unrest experiences of the authors. It related to socialization in a particular subsociety (e.g., student, faculty). It considered certain attributes of the subsociety and considered these attributes within a specific time and place.

*Selected literature.* Throughout this study, the term "selected literature" was used to refer to the literature selected for review in Chapter III.

*Societal.* Throughout this study, the term "societal" referred to the existence of certain social factors originating off campus that related to national and international situations.

*Sociology of knowledge.* The sociology of knowledge referred to the study of "knowledge" as it relates to interacting factors of mind and society. As used here the concept refers to a perspective which is critical of all explanations. Specifically, the position adopted suggests that explanations may reflect selective awareness or use of "facts" and that this selectivity may stem from a person's background or role in the situation.

*Student activists.* Students had been active in some form of protest prior to 1968. Examples of some forms of active student protest prior to 1968 may be found in the writings (Barzun, 1969; Feuer, 1969; Herr, 1974). However, throughout this study, the term "student activists" confines itself to those students who were active in protesting to institutional authorities about a situation having on- or off-campus origins (or both). In short, student activists were the student components of student unrest.

*Student unrest.* Throughout this study, the term "student unrest" referred to an activity rather than a state of mind. Student unrest connoted the existence of a group of students who were similar in behavior and who sought, in some collective manner, to make known to institutional authorities and to the public their opposition to an existing situation . Their behavior was considered unacceptable by the institutional authorities and segments of society.

Within the above context, student unrest referred to overt practices by college students in the United States (1968–1970). These overt practices hindered the normal activities of specific colleges where they took place.

*Subculture.* As used in this study, the term "subculture" pertained to the value/mores system of a particular subgroup. The members of this group may or may not have had values similar to a significant segment of the larger society. Secondary and "current" (1968–1970) socialization to the subculture may have influenced how individuals viewed events that were also viewed by the larger society.

## Research Procedure and Design

The process of researching data relevant to the design and the purpose of this study took the form of a literature search. Bibliographies, book reviews, articles, *Books in*

Chapter II

*Print, Cumulative Book Index,* works cited by authors, indices and readings of educational and sociological learned journals, New Left, SDS and activist publications, plus correspondence to various authors and organizations provided an abundance of data and referrals.

The investigatory procedure sought to ascertain how the authors viewed student unrest. The literature was selected in the following manner:

1. The literature would be in book form.
2. The book would have a single author.
3. The author would have been an observer of sorts, or in some way involved, or present at a campus while the climate of student unrest was still existent.
4. The data of publication of the literature would be as proximate to the event as possible.

Selection of literature according to these criteria ensured, at least in theory, that the authors reviewed had the opportunity to develop views based upon their recent experiences. It also excluded problems of compromise sometimes confronted by multiple authors. Authors who were "on the scene" were selected because of their interaction with the social situation of student unrest.

## SUMMARY

In this chapter, the concept of the sociology of knowledge was examined as an approach to studying student unrest. The use of this perspective implied certain methodological limitations on the data to be used. Within this context, procedures were developed to implement such data selection and analysis. This provided particular books to be used as data.

An attempt was made to determine what could be induced from the literature when the literature was examined using the methodology proposed here. The methodology was not concerned with ascertaining the validity and reliability of the explanations. The concern was to see if by taking this writer's perspective we may further understand why a particular author emphasized a particular explanation. The attempt to understand why particular explanations were offered by an author and to determine any association between the author—explanation and involvement—and his work is an approach found in a subsection of sociology. It is called the sociology of knowledge.

To avoid or minimize methodological confusion, the literature was selected for review according to specific criteria and, therefore, was limited in terms of quantity.

# III
# AN ANALYSIS OF THE SELECTED LITERATURE

## Overview

R. W. Fleming (1975) expressed some doubt regarding the accuracy of the writings on student unrest that were published shortly after the events of 1968–1970. He also expressed reservations about the writings of authors who were in some way involved or at least observers. For example, he stated that "those of us who lived through it have long since published our analyses, but in retrospect one wonders how much of what we said was accurate" (p. 8).

Joseph Adelson had similar reservations regarding the writings of the immediate past (1968–1970) and the accuracy of such writings. Adelson (1974) found that the writings on the university revealed several errors. For example, he found that in these writings the future was considered as an extension of the present (1968–1970). Hence, the idea of a war without draft deferment was incomprehensible to many students. Adelson also contended that students at all institutions of higher education were assumed to be a monolithic group and even a subculture. It was further assumed, according to Adelson, that this group or subculture was a reflection of society at large. Finally, Adelson lamented over the lack of objectivity in such writings.

In this chapter, in the review of the selected literature, it was ascertained that the causes of student unrest, as perceived by the authors, could be organized into three broad categories. These were: Institutional Causes, Societal Causes, and Socializational Causes.

This categorization was used to examine the authors' positions and perceptions of the causes. The causes, the categories of causes, and the authors' orientation and involvement were induced from the selected literature. The examination of this selected literature as raw data had primary importance in this study.

There was no attempt made to compare the observations/explanations given by the authors to a set of observations/facts that may be considered valid/objective.

The authors may or may not have discussed more than one cause in their work selected for analysis. Certainly, student unrest is complex and has more than one perspective. For the purpose of this study, however, the authors were grouped according to the cause (or causes) that was given more credence or weight in their writings.

The review and analysis of each of the selected books took into consideration as general guidelines the following factors:

1. The college where the student unrest occurred and when it occurred.
2. The title of the publication.
3. The author of the publication.
4. The synopsis of the publication which considers the authors' perceptions of the events, the issues, and the causes presented.
5. The authors' orientation toward, or involvement in the events of unrest.
6. The conclusions which could be based upon the data provided by the author and the comments, review, and analysis of this writer.

To provide a "setting," each of the causal categories was introduced with background information.

## INSTITUTIONAL CAUSES

### Introduction

It has been established in the preceding chapters and in the above section that the social phenomenon of student unrest has been attributed to many factors. It has also been established that there are questions regarding the quality of proximate research. Within this context of diversification and quality and the complexities of both, several types of causes of unrest were found and categorized. One of these categories considers the role of the institution (i.e., college or university) as one of the causes of student unrest.

*Chapter III*

Student concerns regarding the structure of institutions of higher learning, particularly the administrative and procedural components, were dramatized by student unrest. In fact, both parents and students had concerns about such institutional factors. These common concerns were evident even when parents and students differed over what courses of action should be taken, as is expressed in the following letter from a parent to her son, an activist at Columbia:

> Your aims, as stated, I totally agree with. The gym, I.D.A., Columbia's long-time poor relationship with the community, the faculty's serious abdication of responsibility to a seriously out-of-touch administration and failure to make real contact with students—all these are questionable to my mind.
> 
> I do not go along with stopping activities of a great university and especially not with going into other people's private files. . . .
> 
> We want you to make an extreme civil sacrifice of yourself no more than we want you to make a military one. (Letter, May 5, 1968)

All of the concerns or reasons for protest mentioned in the first paragraph of this letter originated within the university itself. In their discussion of the issues at Columbia, Parsons and Platt (1973) pointed to these same institutional factors. For example:

> At Columbia in 1968, the problems of the uses of the proposed new gymnasium, the degree to which the gym was to be used by the local community and suspicions regarding the research of the Institute for Defense Analysis were the central issues. (p. 341)

The institution's vulnerability to activism regardless of the validity of the issues was another factor in the events of student unrest. In fact, the very action or reaction of an institution toward activists could be an issue which determined the type of unrest as well as causing the particular events.

For example, Rudd (in Lipset, 1971), the SDS leader of Columbia during the April 1968 student occupation of five buildings, viewed the "issues" as ways to precipitate actions. Rudd was critical of the institution and saw the issues as ostensible, symbolic, secondary to the real goal (a new Columbia), and manipulatable. Rudd explained how the SDS used these "issues":

> Let me tell you. We manufactured the issues. The Institute for Defense Analysis is nothing at Columbia. Just three professors. And the gym issue is bull. It doesn't mean anything to anybody. I had never been to the gym site before the demonstration began. (p. xxi)

*Chapter III*

In addition to the factors of structure and vulnerability to activism, it was found by the American Council on Education (1970), in a report by the Special Committee on Campus Tensions, that the more sophisticated and selective colleges were most likely to suffer student disturbances. Yet, according to Peterson and Bilorusky (1971), the size of the college was more significant than its selectivity/sophistication. Peterson and Bilorusky viewed institutional factors of unrest within a demographic context they developed as a critical mass theory. They explained this theory as "the larger the student body, the greater the likelihood of there being a sufficient number (a critical mass) of students wishing to initiate some—almost any—activity from forming a debating team to kidnapping the trustees" (p. 41).

However, editors of *The Chronicle of Higher Education* did not consider the validity of general issues; they did not consider size or selectivity, but pointed to the rights of students as the chief issue. For example, in *The Chronicle of Higher Education*, a frontpage article proclaimed "Colleges Denial of Student Rights Cause of Most Uprisings" (July 24, 1968, p. 1).

Still another position was that students perceived the university as unresponsive to their concerns and demands. The students were, therefore, revolting against institutional policies and procedures perceived as dictatorial. Yet, the students' perception of the institution as such was also disputed:

> But "the student revolt failed," says Professor Cheit, "because the students thought the university was run by an autocratic central administration, it was a revolution based upon a *fictitious premise*" [emphasis added]. (Hechinger, *New York Times*, August 14, 1972, p. 8)

Kruger and Silvert (1975) were highly critical of analyses which focused on the problems of students in adjusting to an impersonal institution. If such analyses were accepted, then, according to Kruger and Silvert, we would lose sight of the credence and content of student demands. For example, they stated:

> Student protest in relation to the educational institutions is explained as a failure to adjust to the depersonalized bureaucratic multiversity. These students, the prognosis runs, are alienated in the anonymous megastructures of the modern universities.... This approach defines student protest as one type of adjustment to an existing system in utter disregard to the content of the student demands. (p. 39)

Campus unrest was first located at large, highly selective private universities. In fact, selective and permissive institutions attracted students leaning toward protest

(Astin, Astin, Bayer, & Bistonti, 1975). Later, however, student unrest spread to universities and colleges unlike those identified as selective and permissive (Astin et al., 1975). Also, campuses most frequently associated with student unrest were multiversities. These multiversities shared similar educational, social, and political characteristics which, according to Scott and El-Assar (1969), led to student unrest.

The analyses presented above have pertained to a variety of factors and issues ranging from the inherent vulnerability of the university to activism to size and sophistication of the study body. What is common to all these explanations is their focus upon factors that originate within the university itself. In the following analysis of the selected literature a closer look at such institutional causes of unrest is presented.

## Selected Literature

*College*—State University of New York, Buffalo

*Title—The Leaning Ivory Tower*

*Author*—Warren G. Bennis

Warren G. Bennis was Acting Vice President and Vice President for Academic Affairs at the State University of New York at Buffalo during the period of student unrest in 1970. In *The Leaning Ivory Tower*, Bennis identified himself as a college administrator who was involved in student unrest and on the scene. His natural concern was his administrative responsibility and role in the student unrest at SUNY Buffalo. He explained his perspective as an administrator attempting to find a truth or meaning in a situation that involved him in a decision-making role.

The most significant reasons that Bennis gave for the writing of *The Leaning Ivory Tower* pertained to varied kinds of truth—truth that was observed and truth that was participative. From the beginning of his book, Bennis demonstrated awareness of the influence of his decision-making role upon his view of the truth about the events at SUNY Buffalo. Specifically, he asks: "Could I, writing as an actor integrally related to the action I was describing, broaden if not transcend the freedom of thought which our social institutions tend to limit and confine?" (Bennis, 1972, p. viii).

Bennis stated that SUNY Buffalo had a student population of 24,000. Of the 24,000, only 100 or so were classified by the administration as being activists, a figure which Bennis considered accurate. Bennis maintained that the activists' concerns and the issues were: SUNY Buffalo's defense contracts, the federal government's ongoing defense research being conducted on campus, the presence of

*Chapter III*

the Reserve Officers Training Corps on campus, the racism that he terms "alleged," and the student activist demands for an expanded student participation in governance. Bennis did not cite evidence to support his analysis of the concerns and issues. He assumed that the events were documented elsewhere and that he was knowledgeable of them due to his administrative role. His purpose in writing this book was not to prove the existence of these issues and concerns, but to focus on his blame or responsibility for them. He did not question the issues cited, nor offer alternative explanations by other persons that may have also been involved on the scene. Bennis, however, did state his awareness that the issues at SUNY Buffalo were similar to issues on other campuses throughout the United States.

According to Bennis, the undisputed events were based on the issues outlined previously. Within that context, on February 24, 1970, demonstrators threw rocks at the office of the president of SUNY Buffalo. Bennis reported that by March 7 there had been need of medical attention for a total of 125 persons including police, students, and "others." Bennis then cited campus property damage as being in excess of $300,000. He also stated that after the Kent State killings on May 4, 1970, there was almost unchecked disruption and that students and Buffalo police fought on the streets for five days and five nights (Bennis, 1973).

Throughout *The Leaning Ivory Tower*, Bennis reflected over his decision to leave the campus in the midst of the spring crisis. He told of his candidacy for the office of president of Northwestern University and explained that his desire to secure this position motivated him to leave SUNY Buffalo at this time. Bennis repeatedly spoke of his opposition to the SUNY Buffalo administrative plan to request on-campus Buffalo police action against the students and demonstrators. Since he had flown to Evanston, Illinois, for an interview, he was off campus and unable to continue to oppose calling of police for round-the-clock occupation of SUNY. He questioned the wisdom of his decision to leave the campus rather than to continue to advise against police action. Bennis wondered how a social scientist involved in such a social situation could acquire the detachment necessary to make the most objective and moral choice.

Following the administrative decision to call in the police, Bennis resigned as Acting Executive Vice President before the end of the spring semester. This resignation was, according to Bennis, his way of expressing opposition to the administration for this decision. He resigned his other position, University Vice President for Academic Affairs, in August 1970.

*Chapter III*

Bennis' discussion focused on injuries to persons, damages to property, and the impact of seeing one's home of academia in physical and mental anguish. He felt that institutional factors were the significant cause and also the catalyst for student unrest at SUNY Buffalo. Although both the size of the student body and the particular issues were common to other large universities which saw unrest, Bennis thought that the events at SUNY Buffalo were precipitated by the specific manner in which the issues were addressed by the administration. Bennis thought that the call for police action on campus was an administrative overreaction. He further criticized the administration for failing to have meaningful dialogue with the students. In other words, Bennis viewed failure to negotiate as a failure to communicate on the issues with either student or faculty groups. Such overreactions and failures enabled a situation with a small group of dissidents to become escalated and take the form of the events mentioned. The Griener Report, cited by Bennis, also gave the administration a significant share of the blame for the unrest.

Bennis was desirous of becoming a university president and had applied for such a position (while still vice president at SUNY) at Northwestern, the University of Cincinnati, and SUNY Buffalo. His ambition and interest in college administration, and his concern for his status in the eyes of the reader were apparent as he discussed his actions during the time of student unrest. He primarily concerned himself with the function of a university administrator (p. 1) and his specific role and moral responsibility in dealing with student unrest. Hence, we can discern that Bennis' orientation was that of an administrator concerned with both professional ambitions and roles. His purpose in writing *The Leaning Ivory Tower* was described as follows:

> This book is the result of an elephantine year spent contemplating my former life as an administrator at the State University of New York at Buffalo. In it, I have tried to reveal something of the inner workings of an American university in the 1970's, an institution whose outer shell is familiar enough but whose daily administrative life has been clouded by a great information void. A gentleman's agreement protects the privacy of university administrators. Like most other bureaucrats, they tend to be secretive about their work, even when being secretive serves no obvious purpose, even when it is counterproductive. After working uncomfortable within the limits of this restrictive code for a number of years, I am convinced that it calls out for violation. One of the purposes of this book is to show why. (p. 1)

Bennis professed to be a social scientist as well as an administrator. His purpose in writing *The Leaning Ivory Tower*, as well as his recall of the events and his assessment of them, are indicative not only of his involved role, but also his endeavors to transcend it in his reflections.

*Conclusion.* Bennis found that the overreaction of the administrators, their lack of restraint in resorting to police action, and most significantly their failure to communicate with students over the issues were major factors in unrest. Such institutional policies caused the particular form of student unrest that occurred at the State University of New York at Buffalo.

It was found by this writer that Bennis' purpose in writing *The Leaning Ivory Tower* was to use his involvement in, and perceptions of, the events to illustrate how institutional factors caused student unrest. His view was that of an administrator who deplored the situation and attempted to be "objective" in his analysis. This writer concluded that Bennis' role influenced both his perceptions of the causes as institutional and his rationale for writing.

*College*—California State College, Fullerton

*Title*—*How to Kill a College*

*Author*—Cy Epstein

Epstein was a graduate of Yale Graduate School and held the position of Assistant Professor of English at California State College at Fullerton. His experiences during the spring semester of 1970 were the chief subjects of *How to Kill a College* (1971). Epstein was an observer of events on campus, a faculty advisor to the Student Mobilization Committee and a participant in some of the events. He also spent a week as an inmate of Orange County Main Jail because of charges resulting from his role in the disturbances.

The Student Mobilization Committee, as discussed by Epstein, concerned itself with the need of more student participation in governance of the California system of higher education, in general, and the California State College campus, in particular. The Student Mobilization Committee was also concerned with the social issue of the United States involvement in the Vietnam War.

In *How to Kill a College,* Epstein emphasized the frustration of students in their attempts to gain dialogue with an administration that failed to address their grievances. He cited no sources except his own reflections, and directly related the escalation of disruption to the failure of the administration to heed or consider the student concerns. This relationship was particularly illustrated in his discussion of administrative disciplinary procedures which included per Epstein an assumption of student guilt, an unfair burden of proof on the student, and no recourse to appeal the decision or question the rule.

Epstein cited the following events: On February 9, 1970, Governor Ronald Reagan's campus speech was interrupted by profanities and two students were charged with disrupting an academic convocation; on February 19, 1970, four students occupied the president's campus offices; on February 24, 1970, the Science Building was occupied; on February 25, 1970, the police were called and the students ended their occupation without any violent confrontation; but, on March 3, 1970, the campus hearing on the charges against the two students was disrupted and 155 arrests were made.

Epstein felt that the campus disciplinary actions were procedurally deficient in due process. He cited the archaic procedures, and the various administrative concepts of student rights as institutional factors that created and initiated a hostile atmosphere. In effect, the campus hearing, according to Epstein, would not consider any justification or lenience for the students charged with disruption. Epstein deplored this and found that the students were assumed guilty without the benefit of defense. Epstein also reported that although the procedures for these hearings were time-consuming, they gave the student little time to exonerate himself.

Epstein's background was that of a faculty member, a Yale graduate, and a person sympathetic to leftist causes (evidenced by his role as advisor to the Student Mobilization Committee). He was an active participant in unrest and was incarcerated for a week. His sympathies, involvement, and imprisonment were current factors that may have influenced his belief that the institutional situation at California State, Fullerton, caused student unrest, and that the issues were only catalysts. Epstein cited bureaucratic terminology and the "intransigent, vacillating, isolated or self-contradictory administration" as contributing to unrest (pp. 197-198). Given such an administration, according to Epstein, all that is necessary as catalysts for unrest are a triggering event, a social issue, and a small group of disorganized revolutionaries.

*Conclusion.* Epstein had been involved as a faculty member both in defending student rights for due process and as one of those incarcerated. From the perspective of involved faculty, his analysis of events was highly critical of institutional policies. As seen by this writer, there was an association between his personal role and his criticism of the administration. Organized student protest was conceptualized as characteristic of institutions like California State College, and Epstein's analysis was influenced by his involvement and advocacy of student rights there. It is obvious that his perspective, although different from that of an administrator, led him to be critical of institutional policies similar to those cited by Bennis. Epstein, however, did not attempt to transcend his role nor did he indicate any need to do so. He simply felt that certain catalysts mentioned previously are common on college campuses, and but for the administrative stance taken at California State, Fullerton, the student unrest would not have occurred.

*College*—Yale
*Title*—*Letter to the Alumni*
*Author*—John Hersey

Hersey was both a novelist and a nonfiction writer. During the Yale and New Haven, Connecticut, May Day events of 1970, he was the Master of Pierson College at Yale, a post he had held for five years. In his book, *Letter to the Alumni* (1970), he related that Yale students and its president, Kingman Brewster, had expressed concern over the pending trial of a group of Black Panther party members for murder. In particular, the Yale community questioned the ability of the defendants to get a fair trial. There was to be suspension of classes (left to student/faculty option) in mid-April and a rally on New Haven Green, May 1. This entire plan had the approval of the Yale administration.

Hersey's participatory role in the events plus a general background description of factors leading up to May Day were given in *Letter to the Alumni*. Hersey influenced events through his input into the administration's strategy and efforts to contain and shape the demonstrations. Within this context, Hersey discussed the willingness of Yale to address community concerns. "Of all the elements, the two most important, in my opinion, were the solidarity of the black community and the openness of . . . Yale . . . to change" (Hersey, 1970, p. 131). He perceived the plight of the blacks in the New Haven area as being a source of discomfort to some of the more affluent Yale students.

In *Letter to the Alumni*, Hersey repeatedly emphasized that the administration acted as a cause, a positive cause, of the type of student unrest that was found at Yale during this time. The main issue was what the Yale community could do to ensure justice for the defendants in particular, and the New Haven inner-city residents in general. Specifically, he mentioned the concerns of the administration and community leaders about the type of action that was potential, i.e., violent demonstration.

## Chapter III

Hersey explained how institutional factors such as the role of the administration and President Kingman Brewster's "tuning knob" (Hersey, 1970, p. 30) *caused* this particular type of unrest and also *prevented* it from becoming more violent and kept it within the system. The "tuning knob" was offered as evidence of Hersey's contention that Brewster, in containing one type of potential violence and controlling the space and content of the demonstrations, actually caused the May Day activities.

Hersey's orientation was that of an administrator sympathetic to the issues and purpose of May Day. He dedicated this work to Yale's president, Kingman Brewster, whom he admired for his professional abilities and social concerns. The issues and the relations between Yale and the New Haven black community were potentially explosive. Hersey felt that within his institutional function and role, President Kingman Brewster's empathy and control of the substance of the demonstrations caused a particular type of unrest to evolve.

Although Hersey was both a professional writer and an administrator, throughout this work he referred chiefly to his role as administrator. His book showed his personal concern for the societal issues discussed, and also described his administrative concerns regarding a contained and effective May Day. Hersey combined his orientation as a professional writer appalled by violence and concerned with black issues with his role of sympathetic administrator and sought to show how an institution could affect issues relating to student unrest on campuses during 1969.

Although the nonviolent May Day events were precipitated over issues other than institutional, Hersey felt that institutional structure and leadership could also influence and control the type and degree of unrest that occurred on campus when the issues were academic or social.

> The elements of control . . . were: the stability under pressure of the black community and of Yale's black community; the openness of Yale—and *Brewster was the key figure in this*—to real, and not simply token change [emphasis added]. (p. 130)

Hersey found that May Day was caused by societal concerns, but felt that the actual events took a nonviolent form because of institutional policies. In this analysis the term "cause" included reasons for the specific format of the event. In this sense, the actions of the administration and the leadership of Yale's President Kingman Brewster caused the shape of the events. Other policies could, with similar issues, have precipitated different events.

*Conclusion.* In this analysis of *Letter to the Alumni*, the events were examined according to the information given by Hersey. Hersey's comments focused on institutional policies that influenced student unrest to take a certain shape. He wrote of May Day from the perspective of an involved administrator. His perception of the events was not that of an administrator critical of the institution, nor that of a faculty member critical of the administration and demonstrating against its policies. In other words, Hersey wrote as an administrator who was pleased with the policies of the Yale administration. His background and its influence are evident in the following:

> Most of the students admired Brewster for making the statement ("So in spite of my insistence on the limits of my official capacity, I personally want to say that I am appalled and ashamed that things should have to come to such a pass that I am skeptical of the ability of black revolutionaries to achieve a fair trial anywhere in the United States.") in the first place and then for sticking with it under pressure. I admired him for it, because not only do I share his skepticism with respect to a fair trial for black militants; after my researches for *The Algiers Motel Incident* I am skeptical of the ability of any black person to get a fair trial as any white person in any American court today. (Hersey, 1970, p. 114)

In *Letter to the Alumni*, we have established, according to Hersey, the undisputed and common knowledge of the events of May Day 1970 at Yale. What may be disputed are the causes of the events. We may discern that these specific events as well as the events leading up to them interact with Hersey's involvement and influence his perceptions. For example, since Hersey's involvement was that of a member of the institution's administration, he tended to emphasize how well the situation was handled rather than concerning himself with either the documentation of the events or their interpretation. Hersey's administrative involvement apparently influenced his purpose in writing the book, for his theme was that administrations can provide students with opportunities to express concerns in a nondestructive manner. Furthermore, Hersey's background as a journalist concerned about better social justice for blacks made him sympathetic to student concerns regarding the Black Panther trial. *Letter to the Alumni* indicated a particular perception of the events of the May Day demonstration. This perception stemmed from Hersey's background as a journalist concerned with social issues as well as his involvement (a Master for five years) as a college administrator.

*College*—Harvard University
*Title*—*The Fall of the American University*
*Author*—Adam Ulam

*Chapter III*

In *The Fall of the American University* (1972), Adam Ulam referred to his role as a full professor of government at Harvard University. From this perspective he reported that on April 9, 1969, students occupied University Hall and ejected some university officials by force. After the Cambridge community police forcibly cleared the Hall of demonstrators, 50% to 60% of the students boycotted classes. These general perceptions regarding occupation, police action, and boycott were offered by Ulam as common knowledge. He emphasized that his purpose was not to document the specifics of the demonstration, but to express his belief that any institution of higher learning that becomes involved in social issues will fall. He deplored any such involvement except on a small and undefined scale.

In *The Fall of the American University*, Ulam cited the following as the chief issues of unrest:

1. The presence of a program of the Reserve Officers Training Corps on campus.
2. The anticipated expansion of the medical school that would destroy poor housing and evict its residents.

It is interesting to note that while Hersey maintained that institutional involvement and concern with social issues prevented escalation of student demands at Yale, Ulam claimed that such involvement caused unrest:

> For an institution like the university, minding one's own business is not only a desirable precept but a *necessary* condition of its successful functioning and discharging of its obligations to society as well as its members. And the failure to abide by this maxim has been precisely the *principal cause* of the university's troubles [emphasis added]. (Ulam, 1972, p. 128)

Throughout *The Fall of the American University*, Ulam referred again and again to his contention that the universities should limit their role to the promotion of academic learning and the advancement of knowledge. As a basis for this contention he discussed the dimensions of the Harvard administration's involvement in social issues. He maintained, for example, that the atmosphere of Harvard encouraged such student demonstrations, occupation, and the expanded student participation in the boycott. Ulam stated that the police action was unexpected and came as a surprise to students who had been consistently allowed liberties in past social activities. Ulam felt that not only the activists, but the majority of the student body believed that the Harvard administration would never call in the local police.

Within a broad overview of the events as he perceived them, Ulam failed to comment upon the alleged police brutality and the allegation that the police removed

*Chapter III*                          36

their badges before the "bust." Neither did he consider that the police perhaps were called in quickly to prevent the kind of escalation that occurred at Columbia in April of 1968. Ulam felt that unrest could have been avoided but for the permissive atmosphere created by Harvard's not minding its own business on social issues.

    Ulam's involvement was, according to him, confined to his presence and observations at Harvard University during the unrest. Unlike Bennis, he was not an administrator. His position differed from Epstein's in that Epstein was an untenured assistant professor, and was very much involved in social issues. Ulam, unlike Hersey, was neither an administrator nor a journalist. While Bennis and Epstein both criticized the type of action taken by the college administrations, and while Hersey praised the type of action and strategy taken at Yale, Ulam criticized such action on the part of the institution. He felt that a less involved attitude of the institution would have precluded the need for institutional action and proposed that the role of the university should be confined to academics with the least possible involvement in social issues. Ulam maintained that the action of the administration caused a student demonstration to develop into a confrontation, and that the subsequent action of calling in the police served to escalate the confrontation and gain sympathy for the activists.

    *Conclusion*. In Ulam's *The Fall of the American University*, this writer found that there was a connection between Ulam's role as a secure, observant faculty member and his opinion of minimal involvement of the university with social issues. Since he was neither administratively nor sympathetically involved in the actual events, Ulam was free to make suggestions as to how Harvard *should* have handled the protestors, and to express his opinion that the university should mind its own business.

    The set of events at Harvard interact with Ulam's basic orientation or philosophy on university involvement in social issues. This writer has considered and accepted the contention of Ulam that these events actually did occur, and examined how Ulam viewed and stressed certain facets of them. His perspective was that of a faculty member who was neither responsible for making administrative decisions regarding unrest, nor personally involved in the student actions. Ulam used these events to provide evidence for his theory that limited institutional involvement in social issues must be adhered to—or the university will fall.

    *College*—Harvard University

    *Title*—*The Right to Say We: The Adventures of a Young Englishman at Harvard in the Youth Movement*

# Chapter III

*Author*—Richard Zorza

In his opening comments of *The Right to Say We*, Richard Zorza referred to himself as a "bit player" in the events of student unrest at Harvard University in April of 1969. (These were the same events covered by Ulam.)

According to Zorza, he was a 20-year-old sophomore at Harvard when, in April 1969, University Hall was "occupied" by student protestors. The protestors were, by his account, demonstrating their opposition to the Reserve Officers Training Corps (ROTC) programs found on Harvard's campus. Zorza claimed that the presence of ROTC was a chief issue on campus. The Harvard administration's decision to call in police to rid University Hall of protestors was interpreted by Zorza as a betrayal of the students.

Before giving his reaction to these events, Zorza went into his family background: "My name is Richard Zorza. I am twenty. I came from England to America two years ago and to Harvard a year ago. My father was born in Poland; my mother, in England" (p. 3).

Zorza stated that in spite of student and faculty opposition to ROTC, the Harvard Corporation decided that the final determination regarding this issue would be entirely up to them, and neither students nor faculty would be given a voice. Zorza explained that he responded to this decision "with numbed amazement rather than anger. It seemed impossible that Harvard President Pusey was so out of touch with reality.... He was playing into the hands of the extreme radicals" (p. 50).

According to Zorza, the SDS voted not occupy on the night of April 9 but to wait for a rally the following morning. If enough people gathered, an occupation would be "guaranteed" (p. 54). But Zorza also reported that "the strategy developed in the president's office called for quick police action" (p. 55) after the occupancy by students took place on the afternoon of April 10. The police arrived on campus around 4:00 A.M. of April 11.

Throughout his book, Zorza was very critical of the police. Unlike Ulam, he spent considerable time relating eyewitness accounts of police brutality. He and the student eyewitnesses were particularly critical of the police efforts to remain unidentifiable; for example, one student noticed that the police had taken their badges off. A police officer explained that this was done for safety purposes so they would not catch on anyone. Another policeman, however, gave his badge number when requested by a reporter as "six and seven-eighths" (p. 73).

Zorza described the student reaction to the police action to remove anti-ROTC protestors from University Hall. Harvard, according to Zorza, had a sense of

Chapter III                                    38

community cohesiveness regardless of the diversity of student views on specific issues. Zorza observed that the failure of the administration to handle the sit-in without the inclusion of the police violated this sense of cohesiveness and he condemned the administration for their actions.

> The real trouble with deans and the whole administrative machinery was not their conception of Harvard as something special, . . . the problem was their isolation from the real sources of sentiment and reaction among both students and faculty. (pp. 19-20)

Zorza pointed out that "most of the moderate students were mobilized by issues of 'morality,' the way Harvard dealt with the outside community, and its influence in keeping the war going" (p. 191).

Zorza cast the city bureaucracy and the police into a catalytic role when he dedicated *The Right to Say We* "to City Manager Walter J. Sullivan and the Cambridge Police Department . . . *who made it all possible* [emphasis added]."

*Conclusion.* Zorza's admitted orientation was liberal, he had come from England with "a liberal frame of reference" (p. 14) reinforced at Phillips Exeter Academy. *The Right to Say We* is critical of Harvard's administrative machinery and their lack of regard for social issues that concerned students. For unlike Ulam, Zorza felt that Harvard should be involved in such social issues.

In spite of the fact that these issues were found in other college campuses, Zorza felt that the particular unrest at Harvard was caused by the institutional structure and inflexible administrator attitudes. "Unfortunately, those entrusted with a university's development usually become so emotionally involved in it that unchanging self-preservation often becomes an end in itself" (p. 190).

Finally, Zorza described his own feelings and sense of community regarding the Harvard campus and explained that many moderate students and faculty became involved as a result of their perception of the institutional violation of this community and its subculture.

*College*— Columbia University

*Title*—*Across the Barricades*

*Author*—Richard Rosenkrantz

According to Rosenkrantz, he was a graduate student in journalism at Columbia in April 1968, the time of the sit-in at Avery Hall. Rosenkrantz described his active involvement as a protestor and the extensive notes and tapes he recorded during and immediately after the sit-in. His frame of reference was that of a participant/observer equipped with the interest and tools for a journalistic recording of these events. It should be noted, however, that his report was obviously biased in that his interviews were confined to students who were in the process of occupying Avery Hall.

Throughout *Across the Barricades* (1971), Rosenkrantz was critical of the role of Columbia's administration. He was highly sympathetic to his fellow students and felt that the administration precipitated the sit-in by their inaction on issues. Once the sit-in had occurred this same administration further antagonized the students by calling in the police.

Rosenkrantz felt that unrest was good because with the university shut down there could be no business as usual. Furthermore, he stated that after the sit-in "thousands" now supported the demands of the protestors. He offered a seven-point analysis of the results of unrest as he perceived them:

1. The gymnasium was not to be built as originally planned, and there would be new eviction and relocation procedures.
2. Columbia cut relations with the Institute of Defense Analysis (IDA). There would be no more classified research.
3. The ban on indoor demonstrations was lifted.
4. The six student leaders who were on probation before the sit-ins were taken off probation. Amnesty was then given to three pre-sit-in demonstrators. Also, 400 of the 554 criminal charges that were filed against demonstrators were dropped. After the May 1968 demonstrations, a few were expelled and 25 students suspended.
5. Charges against all demonstrators and residents who were at the gymnasium site and who were arrested before the sit-ins were all drastically reduced.
6. Future discipline procedures would not be controlled by the administration in such a rigid fashion; the right of due process and broader appeal would be respected. Students and faculty would have more of a role in discipline procedures.
7. There would be a general restructuring of departments. The students would have a role in curriculum, materials, hiring, and recruitment.

Rosenkrantz devoted most of his book to a journalistic reporting of the sit-ins, and gave little attention to direct analysis of the issues themselves. Yet, his feelings about the causes and issues were implicit in his reporting and in his description of the issues and police action.

*Conclusion.* Rosenkrantz's frame of reference was that of a graduate student with a journalistic background. His status as a student and his interest in recording the events were evident throughout his work. Rosenkrantz gave the most causal emphasis to institutional factors such as the administration's overall handling of the student demonstrations as well as their prior dealings with the issues and students.

In what he termed the "postlog," Rosenkrantz claimed that due to the support of thousands of students all the demonstrators' demands which related to institutional policies at Columbia were met.

Rosenkrantz's knowledge of the student unrest at Columbia was that of a student involved in the sit-in. The causes he cited for unrest are all related to Columbia's institutional policies. If knowledge is a function of social structure, and the college is a social system, then Rosenkrantz's criticisms may be based on the student subculture.

*College* —Columbia

*Title—The Battle for Morningside Heights: Why Students Rebel*

*Author*—Roger Kahn

In *The Battle for Morningside Heights* (1970), Kahn provided a detailed account of the confrontations between police and members of the Columbia community during April 1968. He told of the students and their sympathizers who occupied Hamilton Hall, Executive Offices of the Law Library, Fayerweather Hall, Avery Hall, and Mathematics Hall during April 23–30, 1968. Kahn also described the lifestyle of the protestors and discussed events that led up to the April 30 police action. The chief issue, according to Kahn, was Columbia's involvement with the Institute of Defense Analysis.

> My sympathies stop abruptly at the point where Columbia contributes freely and blindly to the defense-State Complex.... At least twelve trustees and high executives maintain primary connections to Defense-State; an indeterminate but a substantial number of professors scramble for the establishment's grants. The Columbia faculty hires out to help fashion weapons and tactics while relinquishing the right to say whether these—the fruits of their intellectual pains—are put to just use. (p. 20)

Kahn stated that he lived in an apartment on Morningside Drive near the Columbia campus and began his research while the scars of the April events were still noticeable, both in the emotions of those on campus and in the active procedures of the administration regarding the student demands.

Kahn considered himself a neutralist without bias (p. 19); and in his research interviewed those both pro and con regarding the events of Columbia student unrest,

April 1968. Kahn spent half a year wandering Columbia, talking to students, faculty, administration, Harlem community people, and police. After talking to those with divergent views and after his research into the past and present of Columbia, Kahn concluded that institutional factors were the cause of unrest at Columbia.

Senator Eugene J. McCarthy set the stage for Kahn's discussion of institutional factors at the cause of unrest. McCarthy said:

> Universities are in trouble which is to a large extent of their own making, either because of what they have done or permitted to happen, or because of what they have not done or what they have not prevented from happening. (Kahn, 1971, p. 12)

Kahn told why he felt institutional factors at Columbia had provided the prerequisites necessary for a revolutionary impact on campus:

> In what has become a famous quotation from the left, Tom Hayden is supposed to have said of Columbia, "The one thing we knew we could count on was the continuing stupidity of Kirk and Truman." The judgement is harsh and incomplete. What the SDS could really count on was the irrationality, not of men *but of a structure*. To make their revolutionary impact on campus, the radicals required prerequisites. The student body would best be disorganized. . . . The university authorities and faculty ideally would be involved in planning the Vietnam War. . . . The university administration should be insensitive to the Negro drive for equal status.
>
> Columbia met every prerequisite surpassingly. Its students were disorganized, its faculty did help with war planning, and its administrators were insensitive to the poor people living near the campus. Beyond that, it was a weird autocracy. The president ruled without the advice and consent of the university senate. The faculty was passive. The trustees, under venerable law, could not be professors; educators were excluded from the management of Columbia [emphasis added]. (p. 77)

In his discussion of institutional factors as causes of unrest at Columbia, Kahn expressed concern about the perceptions of Columbia's faculty and administrators and felt that "there is pathetically little understanding among faculty and administration of the way things *really are* [emphasis added]" (p. 29).

Roger Kahn's orientation was that of an experienced professional writer and journalist. Although he had not attended Columbia, he was a resident of the broad Columbia community. He included in this work a background history, as well as biographical and character sketches of the selected persons involved in student

*Chapter III* 42

unrest. He further provided an appendix section related to the issues and containing information on SDS factions, Columbia and other universities' list of war contracts, Columbia's decline in national academic standing (1957–1966), and a Columbia chronology (1754–1969).

*Conclusion.* Roger Kahn combined his reporting techniques, his expertise on personality sketches, and his general knowledge of Columbia and produced a book that gave a chilling "you are there" impression. He captured the fear, anger, and violence that permeated the April 30 police action. Although he was involved in, and concerned over what he saw and heard, he attempted to present perspectives from various groups including community, campus, and police. His original bias (stated many times throughout his book) was that Columbia should not be involved in State - Defense contracts. In his reflections, he criticized Columbia and concluded that the actions of the administration caused the student unrest and anti-Columbia interrelated set of ideas.

Further, Kahn found that most demands framed by the Columbia activists were realized. His analysis of the student victories in these demands was remarkably similar to Rosenkrantz's. As mentioned previously, Rosenkrantz was a student of journalism, rather than a professional writer. Rosenkrantz, unlike Kahn, was a participant in the sit-in and only interviewed persons that were sympathetic to the students. Despite these differences, Kahn and Rosenkrantz reached similar conclusions in their criticisms of the Columbia administration. Kahn, however, also found that Columbia was so inflexible that the students could only effect change through forceful confrontation.

*College*—Columbia University
*Title*—*The Strawberry Statement:*
    *Notes of a College Revolutionary*
*Author*—James Simon Kunen

*The Strawberry Statement* is a diary in book form, a record of Kunen's involvement and his thoughts about the issues and events of student unrest at Columbia in April 1968. Kunen characterized the Columbia events (which have been discussed previously) as an "uprising of students against the administration of their school" (p. 173). As it will be shown, Kunen was highly critical of Columbia's administration, yet, he was also ambivalent about his feelings toward specific administrators. Kunen had been a participant in the April 1968 events, and was also a commentator on the sit-in. In his role as commentator he interviewed Herbert Deane, Dean of Columbia. (Deane had inspired Kunen to title his book *The Strawberry Statement*.) Subsequent to his interview, Kunen wrote in his diary—later his book—"God, what am I to do? I *liked* Dean Deane" (p. 135).

As indicated above, Kunen's subtitle to *The Strawberry Statement* was *Notes of a College Revolutionary*. He had, in fact, been arrested for his participation in the sit-in at Hamilton Hall. Kunen's sense of humor regarding this and other events was evident throughout his diary. When Kunen was arrested, subsequent to his activities in occupying Hamilton Hall, the Law Library, and Mathematics Hall, he was put into a police van. During his ride to a nearby precinct, he later admitted he found joy in tearing up a cigarette butt and throwing the particles through the tiny screened window. Kunen recalled the pleasure of littering from a police van. Such a sense of the humorous side of events was not evident in the writings of either Rosenkrantz (1971) or Kahn (1970).

The pleasure of littering from a police van was just one indication of Kunen's personal style and youthful perspective. Indeed, Kunen maintained a dry humor that was aimed at the authorities throughout his diary. Furthermore, Kunen was able to see his own position regarding the United States and his role as revolutionary in a more sympathetic and humorous light than any of the authors previously discussed. Consider the following:

> Since the First Republic of the United States is one hundred ninety-two years old, and I am nineteen, I will give it one more chance. (p. 175)

> I want the cops to sneer, and the old ladies to swear and the businessman to worry. I want everyone to see me and say "there goes an enemy of the state," because that's where I'm at, as we say in the Revolution. (p. 86)

Kunen's attention was directed toward institutional factors of unrest and he maintained throughout his diary that actions by Columbia's administrators and institution-policies prior to the April sit-ins were causes of the demonstrations. Students, according to Kunen, were against the school's association with the Institute for Defense Analysis, a war research organization. The students also perceived Columbia as an elite bastion representing the antithesis of the lifestyle found in the neighboring Harlem community. The university was planning a new gymnasium in Morningside Park which the Harlem community would be allowed to use. However, the facilities open to the community would be separate from those used by the students. As Kunen stated:

> At Columbia, a lot of students simply did not like their school commandeering a park, and they rather disapproved of their school making war, and they told

*Chapter III*

other students who told other students, and we saw that Columbia is our school, and we will have something to say for what it does. (p. 81)

At the time of his writing, Kunen was a 19-year-old student at Columbia whose interest lay in journalistic writing. He was also involved, both as an interviewer and a participant, in the April 1968 sit-ins. In his recall of the events he indicated a sense of community and allegiance to Columbia. The institutional policies and actions of the administrators seemed, according to Kunen, to have violated this sense of community. So, the campus community reacted by becoming more sympathetic to the protestors and provided them with a solid and supportive backing.

The students were determined to have a voice in institutional matters and Kunen thought that such additional student input was both necessary and inevitable. In his diary, he reflected upon a July 1968 discussion with Dean Herbert Deane regarding the original Strawberry Statement:

On April 24, 1967, the Strawberry Statement sprang from the lips of Dean Deane, to absolutely no effect whatever. . . . "A university is definitely not a democratic institution" Professor Deane began. "When decisions begin to be made democratically around here, I will not be here any longer." Commenting on the importance of student opinion to the administration, Professor Deane declared, "Whether or not students vote 'yes' or 'no' on an issue, is like telling me they like strawberries." I like strawberries. But July 30, 1968, didn't stop with the reading of the Strawberry Statement anymore than April 24, 1967, stopped with the pronouncement of it. (p. 140)

Throughout *The Strawberry Statement* it was evident that there was a definite spirit of mission and peer affiliation that increased as the sit-ins grew and continued. However, perhaps Kunen gave too much credit in his diary to the effects of such kinship. The Harvard administration, for example, had called in police a few hours after the April 1969 sit-in, recalling that Columbia had waited too long and allowed for the build up of student sympathy and support. But, neither Harvard's nor Columbia's policies had success.

Kunen does not say much about his background, except that he was a student, a participant, and a writer, and was present during the events. He also explained that although he was on the SDS mailing list, he was not an active member of that organization.

*Conclusion.* It has been considered that there is a connection between those policies criticized by Kunen and the student unrest at Columbia. In other words, the attitude of the Columbia administration produced policies that caused students to demonstrate. The same attitude of Columbia caused them to react to these demonstrations in such a way that brought police on campus and provided more sympathy for the student concerns. In understanding Kunen's comments, attention should be paid to the effect of his resentment of these policies and actions upon his judgment. For in *The Strawberry Statement* this resentment is presented in conjunction with the analysis of how administrative policies caused and gave shape to the sit-ins at Columbia.

It may be concluded that all three of the writers on Columbia were more liberal than conservative. Kunen's comments, quoted here, R. Kahn's bias against the IDA, and Rosenkrantz's criticism of the administration's conservative stance regarding the issues are all examples of liberal leanings. All of these authors were critical of Columbia's administration.

However, a liberal stance does not make a person anti-Columbia and pro-SDS. Horowitz (1969) has criticized liberals who were not sympathetic to the activists as having a vested interest in the universities, and, therefore, being unwilling to oppose the administration. The most important commonality, therefore, that may be found among these three writers is that they were professional or student journalists (and not part of the Columbia administration) who found that the police conducted (at the request of the administration) what was considered to be a final violation of the academic community.

*College*—San Francisco State

*Title* —*The Long Walk at San Francisco State*

*Author*— Kay Boyle

Boyle was a professional writer of fiction, nonfiction, and poetry. In 1968 she was on the faculty of San Francisco State, in the English Department. She recorded the events of student unrest initially in a journal, which later became the basis for her book, *The Long Walk at San Francisco State* (1970).

The comments of this writer focused upon Boyle's report of the events that transpired during the faculty and student demonstrations and the strike at San Francisco State. The strike, as described by Boyle, occurred between November 1968 to March 1969. Also included in her book, but not relevant to this study, were Boyle's notes taken during the trial of Huey Newton. Boyle noted that the students' demands had been:

1. The removal of the Reserve Officers Training Corps from the San Francisco State campus.

*Chapter III*

2. The broadening of the admission goals of the college for black or third-world students.
3. The hiring of faculty having a similar black or third-world ethnic background to teach special courses.

Boyle went on to explain that the presence of the much opposed Reserve Officers Training Corps represented the institution's involvement in the Vietnam War. She found that the institution was not responding to the needs of minority groups seeking admission, and also that such minority students' needs would be better served by having special courses, such as Black Studies, taught by blacks. The students reasoned, according to Boyle, that such faculty could have better knowledge and empathy with course content and also relate better to the students.

Boyle was highly critical of the administration throughout this work, especially of their handling of the issues. For example, she deplored the climate of oppression and broken promises and attributed both to the administration. She described (in addition to the Black Studies broken promises) the violence directed against the students, the arrests by the San Francisco policemen, and the use of the tactical police force to close the college.

One interesting event, which Boyle highlighted occurred on December 2, 1968. During a demonstration, President Hayakawa of San Francisco State pulled the wires out of an audio apparatus being used by student protestors. Boyle then called him "Eichmann" and Hayakawa shouted that Boyle was "fired." (Hayakawa had been appointed to his position after the abrupt resignation on November 26, 1968, of Robert R. Smith.) Hayakawa ordered the sound truck off campus and then climbed on top of it and yanked out the wires from the loudspeakers.

One of the reasons why Hayakawa was selected as acting president was because of his conservative ideas regarding student demands and actions. Boyle, by her interests and regards over student demands and concerns, could hardly be considered partial to such a conservative stance. Hayakawa and Boyle differed about the role of the institution in strikes and how student demands should be viewed and implemented. As Hayakawa stated:

> The universities and colleges should be centers for the dissemination of the values of our culture and the passing on of those values. But, dammit, with enough half-assed Platos in our university departments, they are trying to make of them centers of sedition and destruction. (Orrick, 1970, p. 63)

*Conclusion.* Based upon Boyle's criticism of institutional policies and their implementation, and related to her sympathy (ironically, some of this shared by Hayakawa) toward student concerns, Boyle perceived that the failure to listen to student demands led to the constant unrest at San Francisco State. Her concern in writing this book was to show (rather than sociologically analyze) the agony of the experience of unrest.

Boyle, like Hersey (1970) and R. Kahn (1970), was a professional writer. Unlike Hersey, she was not an administrator; and unlike Kahn, she was not simply a member of a campus community at large, neither did she maintain that she was an unbiased observer. Boyle was on the scene as a professional writer and a member of the faculty. Her orientation was one that indicated sympathy to the concerns of the students. Although Boyle was aware that such concerns were found on other campuses, she felt that institutional factors were the cause of the specific unrest at San Francisco State.

**Summary**

Based upon the literature selected for review under "Institutional Factors," it was found that students resented some institutional policies. This resentment was based upon the interconnectedness between the oppressed stratum (as the students perceived themselves) and the institutional power in areas having a definite differentiation of value orientations. In the sociology of knowledge, it is stressed that such an awareness of resentment, based upon value orientations, helps us to understand and interpret such a social phenomenon as student unrest. What is called the value-generating function of resentment was developed by Mannheim (1952):

> One could say in the case of Christianity, it was resentment which gave the lower strata courage to emancipate themselves, at least physically, from the domination of an unjust system of values and to set up their own in opposition to it. (p. 25)

In this section, the authors were found to have cited the institution as a significant (but not necessarily exclusive) cause of student unrest. It was further shown that parents as well as students were resentful toward institutions of higher learning.

In addition to criticisms of institutions, there was also disagreement on how to address such criticisms. Parson and Platt (1973) stressed that institutional policies were issues of legitimate concern, but Rudd (in Lipset, 1971) stated that institutional policies helped activists manufacture issues, thus indicating the institutional impotence during a crisis.

*Chapter III*

The institutions were criticized for either bringing in police too late or too early, and also for displaying too much social concern or too little. Authors faulted both administrative policies and their implementation.

Bennis (1973), Epstein (1971), Ulam (1972) were either faculty members or a college administrator, and all found fault with the specific institution. Epstein, who was incarcerated and sympathetic to students, criticized the attitude of the administrators for not listening to student concerns. (From the literature, it was found that Ulam was higher both in age and faculty rank than Epstein.) Bennis was an administrator who continually examined his role and was introspective about how institutional policies were implemented.

Kunen (1970) and Rosenkrantz (1971) were students at Columbia. Zorza (1970) was a student at Harvard. All three were appalled by police action and all three found the administration's positions and their treatment of students to be causes of student unrest.

Boyle (1970) and Hersey (1970) were professional writers and were of the staff of the institution about which they wrote. Boyle blamed the acting president of San Francisco State and the institutional policies for the student demonstrations, the strike, and the violence. R. Kahn (1970) who was also a professional writer, but not connected with Columbia except demographically, concurred with Boyle. Hersey also found the president and institutional policies instrumental in causing the particular (and to Hersey, positive) type of May Day demonstration student unrest at Yale.

It was found that the above authors were students, professional writers, and faculty or staff. As induced from the literature, all the above authors cited the role of the institution as a cause of student unrest at the institution about which they wrote. Furthermore, all were in some way involved in the events of student unrest.

The institution has many aspects of a social system and, as such, it represents those in power. Given such representation, the institution was criticized for both representing and maintaining the status quo. All of the selected authors perceived the college as having an interrelated system of norms and roles and an organized policy to implement them. Perceptions differed, however, on value orientations toward the system and the manner in which the institutional agency either strengthened or weakened those norms and roles.

An institution has a careful delineation of roles which are perceived according to the definition of the situation. In student unrest, the definition of the situation could vary depending upon the perception of the activists, administrators, and the selected authors. Although some authors were critical of activists and others were critical of administrators, all of these authors perceived the roles played by the institution's administrators as causing student unrest. This perception transcended the background of these authors.

The selected authors in this section found that student unrest was a symptom of the ills of higher education. Both Bennis (1973) and Boyle (1970) were critical of the roles played by the administrations. Hersey (1970), however, took the unique view that the administration caused a type of unrest that was the lesser evil; and but for Yale's President Kingman Brewster, the form of unrest as well as its substantive factors would have been a far greater evil. Epstein (1971) and Roger Kahn (1970) were highly critical of administrative stances and procedures, while Ulam (1972) was also highly critical of procedures. Ulam, however, thought that the solution should have been for the university to mind its own business. The main thrust of the two other authors, Kunen (1970) and Rosenkrantz (1971), was that the institution was violating the students' concepts of community as well as their subcultures. Zorza (1970) was in agreement with all of the above excepting Ulam.

Finally, a position similar to Krueger and Silvert (1975) was advanced by Douglas Sloan in his comments pertaining to student unrest in the 60s:

> Students . . . attacked only the service station ethic of the university, and not its underlying conception of knowledge, which the students in large part shared. Consequently, it was possible to deny rather successfully that the student criticisms in any way called into question the fundamental nature of the university. (Sloan, 1978, p. 333)

At this point, one may summarize that the role of the institution was viewed from different perspectives of the situation and that such general perspectives were used regardless of the role the authors had to the institution. Evaluations of the situation also varied with no consistent pattern of association with the author's role in the institution.

## SOCIALIZATION CAUSES

**Introduction**

Socialization has an influence on future role performance which, in turn, has a bearing on group or subculture approval. In this study of student unrest, socialization was viewed from the concept of interaction. A person involved in student unrest could interact in a positive or negative manner to the activists or to those opposing the activists. Opposition could be based upon either the goals or methods of the activists.

If a person's socialization is toward a subculture that favors student unrest, certain behavioral patterns will follow. Quite naturally, if a person's socialization is toward a

*Chapter III*

subculture that is opposed to student unrest, different behavioral patterns will follow.

According to Horowitz (1969):

> It is clear that this generation has the time and the affluence to see itself as a *social subclass* having permanent political and social aims, even though the state of being a student is transitional [emphasis added]. (p. 553)

Braden (1971) reinforced the idea that the sociology of knowledge may be a factor in viewing causes of student unrest:

> It is probably a waste of breath why they [Flacks and Bettelheim] argue a specific issue: their point of view on any subject is colored or even predetermined by their *Weltsansicht* of their basic apprehension of reality as a whole. (p. 30)
>
> I [Bettelheim] think that everybody's concern with this movement—including my own, and Professor Flack's—is conditioned by his own upbringing, his own childhood, and his own life experience and what he brings to them. (p. 60)

The above quotes indicate that a person's upbringing fits into the category of socialization factors in student unrest as well as the perception of student unrest. As defined in Chapter II, socialization was specified to consider influences that come from family, peers, and (later) institutional colleagues.

Academia offers a new stage of socialization for the faculty, the students, and the administration. And, depending in part on factors mentioned previously by Bettelheim (Braden, 1971, p. 60), it means different things to different authors. Because of the many variables involved in the student, the faculty, and the administration orientations and their actions, socialization is significant; but it cannot totally account for the development and the actions of authors of the selected literature. However, a specific "student unrest" commonality (found to be present in the activists *both* left and right) would signify a subculture, especially a student subculture (Shimahara, 1975). Such a subculture would be a factor in current secondary socialization.

For the purposes of analyses, the current and secondary socialization concepts were taken to have two agents that interacted within the subculture:

1. The social system of the college.

2. The voluntary associations both intrinsic and extrinsic to social system.

Boulding's (1971) research into the relationship between socialization and student attitudes is relevant to the concept of socialization and to the literature analyzed in this section. It was listed specifically in the following quote taken from her conclusion:

> Six agents of socialization were identified . . . : the family, the primary school environment, the extra-familial role models, the school, the secondary social

environment, and voluntary associations. It was suggested that the relative importance of each agent would shift over time, moving from family primary in childhood to secondary social environment and voluntary associations in young adulthood. It was also suggested that key public events in late childhood and early adolescence would contribute critically to the shaping of the world view during a period when basic cognitive introduction of social facts was going on, and would persist over time without allowing the same primacy to later public events. (pp. 40-41)

Socializing agents were indicated to interact in various degrees depending on student involvement on campus during or immediately following student unrest.

Krueger and Silvert (1975) maintained all psychological explanations of student unrest thus far advanced, regardless of whether they are sympathetic or unsympathetic to students, "explain away" student concerns. Peterson (1968) found that empirical studies of radical activists have been consistent in finding most activist students coming from the upper middle class and having proliberal or radical parents who practiced permissive child rearing. These radical activists were also found to be highly intelligent. Whether the activists were explained as applying or rebelling against the socialization patterns of their parents, the focus of the analyses was on explaining activist and faculty behavior.

While students were following their bent, which

seemed to be pushing them ever closer to changing the "system" most of their mentors continued unperturbedly to spin their theories within the parameters of the *status quo*, apparently accepting these as the only frames of reference for their scientific discourse. (Krueger & Silvert, 1975, p. 10)

Student unrest has been analyzed from various conceptual frameworks which suggest various ways causes of unrest may be studied. These frameworks include the structural, functional, and the psychological. Socialization is associated with the social structure and any individual role, for it is the process by which social institutions shape individuals to carry out necessary roles. While socialization may relate to the maintenance of an existing social structure, it may also relate to an effort to change an existing social structure.

**Selected Literature**

*College*—Harvard University
*Title*—*Push Comes to Shove:*
*The Escalation of Student Protest*

*Chapter III*

*Author*—Steven Kelman

In *Push Comes to Shove* (1970), Kelman gave an evaluation of the causes and results of the occupation of Harvard's University Hall, April 9, 1969. Kelman stated that he was an undergraduate student at Harvard at that time.

According to Kelman, 419 students occupied a Harvard building to protest the presence of the Reserve Officers Training Corps on Harvard's campus. Kelman maintained that this protest was, in fact, precipitated by a minority of the members of the SDS, who acted in spite of a vote taken by that organization *not* to do so. Kelman was less sympathetic to the SDS than Zorza, and differed in his perception of what happened when the SDS met to decide if and when to occupy. While Zorza maintained that it was understood that there would be an occupation contingent upon crowd support, Kelman stated that:

> Jared Israel took the microphone to say that the debate was not over. *There would be some people who would take over the building tonight no matter what the group decided.* . . . In the official SDS version of the meeting, it is stated that the final vote agreed to take over a building at some randomly selected time during the next week [emphasis added]. (p. 262)

Kelman went on to discuss the mentality and attitudes of SDS members, and deplored their irrational, undemocratic, and unsocialist orientations. He also criticized the apathy of moderate students which allowed the SDS minority to vent their activism on campus. According to Kelman, it was the SDS subculture in conjunction with this moderate apathy which caused the unrest at Harvard. As Kelman states, "The Harvard confrontation would never have been possible without the promotion of a campus atmosphere hermetically sealed from reality" (p. 238). He found that students in the SDS had been socialized by the new and radical left, and that they were in rebellion against middle-class values.

> The intellectual Left Extremists at Harvard . . . were good people. . . . The same cannot be said for the other major social stratum which provides recruits for SDS and the backbone of the new cadres recruited. . . . These are WASP rebels. The sight of an aristocrat who has lost the will to live is esthetically degrading. (p. 145)

By his own account, Kelman was a socialist, an active member of the Young People's Socialist League (YPSL), and a one-time member of the SDS. He found radicals to be just as diverse as middle-class nonradicals, and felt that both groups had, to various degrees, an impatience toward the United States society. He described the extreme radicals as "soft" and not up to prior aristocratic standards. The original SDS members had been "heredity radicals" whose backgrounds oriented them toward change, but not destruction, of United States colleges and society.

Kelman's analysis reflected his sympathy to leftist causes, but he deplored the new SDS members as being upper class and as lacking a respect and interest in traditional socialist methods. His reflections indicate a dislike for the new type member with different orientations. This difference was responsible for the actions of the previously described minority who acted in spite of a vote by the majority, i.e., their expectations to get their own way exceeded any ideological concept of democratic decision making that Kelman had found in the left movement prior to 1969. Kelman's background as a member of the Socialist Party and his respect for the original SDS elite was referred to throughout his work, but he compared the 1969 SDS with the Nazi Party and implied that these new members were sick or at least irrational.

Kelman's analysis was related to socialization (subculture, generational conflict) concepts as advanced by Bettelheim (in Braden, 1971), Boulding (1971), and Feuer (1969). Feuer's theory has the younger generation desirous of the economic and social power held by the older generation. Bettelheim found that the child-rearing process based upon permissiveness could produce disrespect in the young for authority, while Boulding saw the influence of peer socialization increasing.

Kelman's criticism of a new radical movement lacking the "background" found in the traditional socialist movement was based upon his knowledge and involvement with the Young People's Socialist League. For Kelman, the YPSL represented the older and more elite left movement. The antagonism between older and newer groups with apparently similar ideologies was discussed from a different, but relevant perspective by Lorenz (1974):

> Students of the extreme left attack professors of the extreme left almost as frequently as those of the extreme right. Under the leadership of Daniel Cohn-Bendit, Communist students once vehemently abused Herbert Marcuse, making the most absurd allegations, for instance, that he was on the payroll of the CIA. The demonstrators manifestly were not motivated by the fact that he belonged to another political affiliation, but rather by the generation gap.
> In the same subconscious and intuitive way, the older generation *understands* what these ostensible protests really are: insults and aggressivity fueled by hatred. (p. 67)

*Conclusion.* Kelman found that the student unrest was caused by new radicals having different orientations than the original SDS of the YPSL. Both his analysis and what he

*Chapter III* 54

disclosed about his background provided data to conclude that socialization by different subcultures caused the actual form and style of unrest at Harvard. The data provided in this book enabled this writer to view an association between a specific type of socialization and activist orientations. In other words, undergraduates involved with traditional socialist or old left movements had specific ideas about activism which could conflict with the ideas of the students who had no such background. Out of this conflict of orientations arose the specific type of unrest at Harvard, April 1969.

As Kelman concluded:
> It is... no surprise that student revolutionary movements like the SDS, as they become mass forces and, therefore, need to become rooted in student psychological self-interest, lose their positive aspects and degenerate into groups whose effects are destructive. (p. 279)

*College*— Harvard University
*Title—Harvard, Through Change and Through Storm*
*Author*—E. J. Kahn, Jr.

In *Harvard, Through Change and Through Storm* (1969), Kahn mentioned that he had been a graduate of Harvard and that his graduation class, that of 1937, had been of a previous generation.

Kahn described himself as having an interest in writing and experience as a journalist. He returned to Harvard, in the fall of 1967, with the purpose of gathering material for a book about the university, with history as its theme.

Kahn discussed his plans to research and to write on selected historical Harvard topics. The eventual work, which is considered here, had as its main focus the recent history of Harvard. It also contained brief biographical sketches of administrators who were involved in the student sit-in on April 9, 1969. This and other events leading up to the sit-in served as a background for the work.

According to Kahn, during the sit-in approximately 200 students were involved. Of these, 186 were jailed and 40 were injured when Cambridge police cleared the University Hall of demonstrators. Subsequently, 2,000 students called a three-day strike to condemn the administration and the actions of the police. The issues, according to Kahn, were both student and institutional in origin.

E. J. Kahn did not directly analyze the issues or causes of unrest. He did, however, repeatedly refer to the minority of SDS members who decided to sit-in in spite of the SDS vote to hold such action in abeyance. He also developed his ideas about the spirit of Harvard's community by discussing the moderate students who were not SDS members but became sympathetic to the activists after the police action described previously. In his biographical sketches of administrators, and in his reporting on the cohesiveness of the student body, Kahn demonstrated an understanding of the status quo and the goals of the SDS.

Kahn was a generation apart from the Harvard students; in fact, his son was a Harvard undergraduate in 1967-1969. Kahn's presence had as its purpose a book about Harvard, but as it happened he witnessed and used his journalistic ability to record the events of student unrest. His theory was that the students at Harvard, ended up supporting a minority action because of their attachment to the school. In other words, student loyalty to Harvard transcended the original issues.

In spite of their differences in age and orientation, both E. J. Kahn (1969) and Kelman (1970) agreed that the sit-in got support in spite of its being a very minority-type action. Both found that the Harvard community was socialized into having loyalty to a peer and Harvard subculture that transcended personal feelings about the original issues. Throughout his book, Kahn endeavored to show how the student unrest was a reaction to the police action; that demonstrators felt *their* Harvard was betrayed by such action.

*Conclusion.* Kahn gave limited explicit reasoning about the causes of student unrest at Harvard. He did not go into his background in detail. Yet, there was sufficient evidence to show that he reported both the administrators' and the SDS' views. As Kahn perceived it, student unrest was caused by student concerns over ROTC, the plight of the activists involved in the sit-in, and the actions of the police. In other words, subculture concerns caused the students to align themselves against the administration and the police. Hence, Kahn's main interest is in the type and ramifications of unrest rather than the issues. He attempted to show a "spirit" of Harvard based on a tradition of loyalty to peers when confronted by outsiders. As a reporter older than undergraduates, he strived to put the events into a historical perspective.

Kahn's analysis is supported by Spady (1974) who stated that students must have a set of values that support the administrative actions of educational institutions. If student values, developed in part and precipitated by socialization to a particular student subculture, do not support such actions, then these same actions will inevitably be opposed.

Chapter III

*College*—University of California, Berkeley
*Title*—*The Kumquat Statement*
*Author*— John R. Coyne, Jr.

John R. Coyne, Jr., noted that he was a veteran of the United States Marines. After his discharge in 1957 he had written journalistic articles which appeared in *The National Review*. This publication, *The National Review*, is considered by this writer, and, in general, to be a conservatively oriented publication. Although Coyne provided little other information as to his background, the indications are that he was politically conservative.

In 1968, Coyne was a graduate student at UCLA, Berkeley. In *The Kumquat Statement* (1970) he described and criticized the October 1968 bombing of the Berkeley campus NROTC building. Coyne also provided an account of the anti-war student sit-ins at Sproul and Moss Halls during the 1968 fall semester. Later, Coyne identified the same (or similarly ideological) group of students involved in the sit-ins as being participants in the "people's park" battles that occurred in the city of Berkeley. According to Coyne, the police sought to free the park from trespassers who initially camped there and had many demonstrations against the war, and then against anyone who sought to remove them from the park.

*The Kumquat Statement* focused upon the concepts of rebellion and subculture. As Coyne perceived them, the issues were the Vietnam War and whether lectures by Eldridge Cleaver on campus warranted course credit. Coyne also discussed the causal role of the New Left and the Black Militants, and found that these two groups were quite active on the Berkeley campus.

Coyne felt that the New Left and Black Militants served as reference groups for activists who desired to stop the Vietnam War and to foster the goals of blacks by means that would be violent if necessary. The activists had been socialized, in other words, by a subculture whose goal it was to change the role Berkeley had been playing regarding the Vietnam War and certain minority-oriented course offerings. As a result of this socialization, student activists responded to the exhortations of those groups who wished to use the campus as a platform to launch and publicize the need for radical change.

It is worthwhile here to consider the following clarification of "reference group":

> Because of the differentiated character of modern mass societies, the concept of reference group, or some suitable substitute, will always have a central place in any realistic conceptual scheme for its analysis. As is pointed out above, it will be most useful if it is used to designate that group whose perspective is

assumed by the actor as the frame of reference for the organization of his perceptual experience. Organized perspectives arise in and become charged through participation in common communication channels, and the diversity of mass societies arises from the multiplicity of channels and the ease with which one may participate in them. (Shibutani, 1955, p. 569)

It should also be noted that Warren (1968) stressed that any subculture, regardless of its reference group, should not be perceived as a separate entity, but as an element in the overall intellectual, vocational, and socializational process. Based upon Coyne's comments, especially about the New Left, he claimed that students, especially the New Left, were responsible for the events of unrest because they had been socialized by a radical subculture and referred to radical left and black movements. Coyne perceived the militant groups as acting in a manner based upon their socialization and as helping to radicalize other students with similar leanings by acting as a reference group for them.

*Conclusion.* Coyne (1970) was a student like Kelman (1970), although older; and had been a journalist like E. J. Kahn, but younger and more conservative. Coyne pointed to socialization of students by activist groups as the cause of unrest at the University of California at Berkeley. The criticisms of Kelman and Coyne, although based upon different ideological perspectives and directed at liberal student groups at different colleges, were quite similar. Both authors perceived a minority group using demonstrations and confrontation for change.

**Summary**

This section concerned itself with secondary socialization and with the college community having different subcultures and reference groups within its framework of a social system. The books considered covered student unrest at the University of California, Berkeley, and Harvard University.

Two of the authors, Coyne (1970) and E. J. Kahn (1969) were journalists. They were older than the average undergraduates and were outsiders to the usual college community. (Specifically, Kahn was older and Coyne more conservative.) In contrast, Kelman (1970), who wrote about Harvard, was an undergraduate at Harvard. He was also the most liberal. In spite of this liberality and involvement, he takes a position which is perhaps more characteristic of outsiders. Kelman found that the new type member (i.e., non-elite) of the SDS subculture and the moderate students' apathy caused the student unrest at Harvard in April 1969. Kelman also found that the sense of a Harvard community transcended the ideological differences of the radicals, moderates, and other groups on campus. This sense of Harvard community further caused an integrated process of interaction and unification in protest against the actions of a "stranger" group, i.e., the police, on campus. In this particular instance, the protestors were socialized more toward their Harvard community identity and less toward distinct ideologies. E. J. Kahn's (1969) book had similar conclusions; and in spite of a generational difference between himself and the undergraduates, it was obvious that he too had an attachment to a "we" feeling regarding the Harvard community.

A person is socialized in reference to a particular group. The children, for example, of radicals or left-wing-oriented parents are assumed to have been exposed to a certain set of values based upon these orientations. Hence, the term "red diaper babies" has been used to describe student activists who had as parents left-wing persons. It should be also considered that socialization is a relative term that takes on a specific meaning when it is used in reference to the norms and expectations of a specific group or subculture.

Socialization as a cause of unrest could be related to a positive view of subculture socialization of student activists, or it could be related to the theory that classifies activists as impatient and immature. In discussing the inner causes of student unrest, Mehnart (1976) stated that:

> The inability to wait, the desire to have "everything at once," no matter what—psychologists like to trace this back to the parents' (especially the mother's) habit of satisfying speedily every wish of their children. David Riesman (*Time*, May 3, 1968) said of the impatiently demanding and rioting students that they had once been the babies who always had to be picked up right away when they cried. (p. 348)

As stated previously, the selected authors wrote about their college experience and involvement with the events of student unrest during the time (1968-1970) of the study. Of these selected authors, only three were categorized into this section on socializational causes. Although all showed agreement that socialization was a cause of unrest, they differed in their perception of the roles of the students and the socialization reference group. In fact, the very concept of socialization was given different meanings by the authors. The more conservative the author (Coyne, 1970), the less positive he is about activist socialization. The most liberal (Kelman, 1970), however, saw positive value in student activism and supported the activist position on the issues. At the same time, this liberal author was critical of new radicals who wanted their own way at the expense of participatory democracy.

In conclusion, very few authors (only three) of the total selected found socialization factors as the most significant cause of unrest. Coyne (1970) and Kelman (1970), although having different background (Coyne right and Kelman left), both found that activists were socialized to expect instant gratification. It should be noted, however, that the activists they were criticizing were socialized by different reference groups. The other author, E. J. Kahn, Jr. (1969), although sympathetic to the activists, was also sympathetic to the administrators. His comments pertained to the particular roles that each group played out as a result of their particular orientation.

## Societal Causes

**Introduction**

Mark Rudd, leader of the Students for a Democratic Society (SDS) during the 1968 student unrest at Columbia, saw the causes of student unrest as societal in origin. Rudd was highly critical of the social characteristics of the United States and considered Columbia as a symbol of a social system that was deplored by the SDS. Brann (1968), in a discussion of Columbia student unrest, found that the institutional issues unfortunately overshadowed the social issues. According to Brann,

> The basic SDS philosophy has received little attention in the "straight press," perhaps obscured by the gym and Dr. Kirk. As Columbia SDS Chairman, Mark Rudd has attempted to explain countless times the SDS is not particularly interested in trying to reform Columbia. SDS wants the entire social order and economic system overhauled. "It is impossible to have an honest university in a basically dishonest society," he often says. He views the Columbia turmoil as a mechanism to educate students and the public to the "corrupt and exploitative" nature of American society. "We're in a pre-revolutionary period, a time of education," he once told me. He and other SDS leaders are fond of comparing our society to a tree which needs new roots, not merely repairs on a branch. Thus, the SDS philosophy is aimed at every major U.S. university, especially those with a plethora of government contracts or those with prestigious schools, such as Columbia's School for International Affairs, which obviously help preserve and promote the established order. (p. 8)

Brann, as shown above, saw societal factors as perceived by the Students for a Democratic Society (SDS) as a cause of student unrest and was concerned about potential unrest on other campuses because of "a general disillusionment among masses of students about the democratic processes and the viability of our society" (Brann, 1968, p. 8).

*Chapter III*

In a book review, Lipset (Summer, 1974) cited what he considered a societal cause. He saw the Vietnam War and how it affected students as having high correlation with student unrest.

> It may be noted ... that the protest only became massive after draft deferments for graduates were cancelled in 1968, and that it quickly began to ebb as the Nixon administration's policy of Vietnamization heralded the withdrawal of troops from Vietnam and sharp declines in draft calls. (p. 57)

Luria and his wife Zelia (in Heer, 1974), maintained that "in the United States student unrest is not so much a revolt against traditional values as a *revulsion against a society* that at times seems to betray its own proclaimed values" (Heer, p. 161). (Emphasis added.)

Erlich and Erlich (1970) also found that "the implications of student protest go far beyond institutions of learning, far beyond the communities in which students live, to the heart of the 'American Mission'" (p. 12).

Hook (September 1976) agreed with Lipset (1974); and in his comments on the student protest movement of the 60s said, "It was inspired primarily not by felt deficiencies in student education but by issues that in their origin had *nothing to do with campus studies*—Vietnam, the draft" (p. 59). (Emphasis added.)

We have illustrated here some of the societal factors cited as possible causes for student unrest. These factors ranged from considering the issues as indicative of an evil society, to the issues being considered as blemishes on a basically good society, and on to issues being inconveniences that could interfere with the education and subsequent careers of draft-eligible students.

There is also to be considered the concept of awareness to social change and divergent value orientations in response to social change. In particular one value orientation would lead groups to oppose the social technocratic direction of mass society. Mehnert (1976), in his study of the radical movements of the 1960s and their legacy called *Twilight of the Young*, found that students are

> apprehensive that, in what Zbigniev Brzezinski, formerly of Columbia University, called the technotronic age, they will be outdated, discarded, shunted off.
> ... Since nothing creates closer ties than facing the same enemy, many prefer groups which stand in opposition to society. (p. 347)

The awareness of differences in value orientations between students and the majority of those having the most input into social policy contributes to a search by students for what Mannheim (Wolff, 1971) referred to as "a search into the new direction of events and into their new requirements" (p. 376).

Some students were critical of society and sought complete change or restructuring. Some resented Vietnam, feared technocracy, and, in general, reacted to factors originating in the social complex and influencing their life on campus.

There was considerable disagreement over how social issues should be resolved. The disagreement related to methods of attacking social problems and fear of backlash. For example, consider the following excerpt of a letter from a parent to her activist son:

> I think our society can be mended... I don't yet see either in theory or in practice a better method to try than representative democracy;... I honestly believe that there is just around the American corner (to appear if moralistic law-breaking becomes more widespread and more frightening to all segments of society) an American police state, a place where the police brutality of Tuesday morning will seem like greasy kids' stuff. (May 5, 1968)

**Selected Literature**

*College*—Columbia University

*Title*—*Radical and Militant Youth*:

    *A Psychoanalytic Inquiry*

*Author*— Robert Libert

Robert Libert was on the Columbia staff in 1968. He was a member of the faculty in the undergraduate section of the Columbia Morningside Heights campus. He was also a student counselor and a consultant for the Columbia Counseling Service. He was on campus during the April 1968 student unrest and was, by his own account, concerned with student behavior in such events.

Libert described *Radical and Militant Youth* as "firehouse research," composed of his personal reaction and interviews which took place while the events were proximate to his memory and the results were evident or still transpiring. Libert dealt with the same events as the previously discussed Columbia authors and his facts are similar to theirs regarding the actual sit-in and police action. Libert pointed to interacting and interrelated forces as factors that caused student unrest. He did, however, relate all factors to the significant societal factors. Libert (1971) found as significant

> interacting forces—character structure, value systems, response to unconscious as well as conscious meaning of the particular radical actions undertaken and the external reality of the immediate sociopolitical situation. (p. 67)

*Chapter III*                    62

Libert stressed the importance of the April 30 police bust that, according to Libert, occurred between 2:00–4:00 A.M. In his opinion, the students resented this impingement of an outside social force, i.e., the police. In this case, the police action represented a society intent upon maintaining a certain social structure regardless of the cost or injuries to students. Consequently the original issues were no longer the main factors. The 6,000 students who sympathized with the demonstrators did so not because they experienced a change of heart about the gymnasium and the war, but because they resented a violation of their campus community by an outside social agency.

Just as in 1964 at the University of California, Berkeley, and at Cornell in 1969, faculty and students became more aware of their resentment. Libert credited this awareness, value orientation, and resentment to those students who first had occupied the five Columbia buildings.

> For the most of the thousand Columbia students who occupied buildings, the action grew out of political and moral judgments based on their understanding of the university with regard to the war, the surrounding community and the students themselves. (p. 215)

Libert focused on societal factors and student awareness of them. As he perceived it, the institution was a part of the larger social system having rules and norms that were opposed by many of the students. He examined student unrest on a social psychology level, and related it to factors in society that transcended the actual institution of the university.

In *Radical and Militant Youth*, Libert emphasized the effect of student unrest on his sampling of the student population at Columbia. However, in his data we find constant allusions by students to the societal dimensions of the effects of student unrest. It is interesting to find both cause and effect in this data.

Libert does not dispute the established facts on Columbia student unrest and cites events that he assumed to be common knowledge and hence found no need to document. However, in his comments on these common knowledge facts we find a focus on societal factors as the chief cause.

*Conclusion.* Libert established that he was sympathetic to students, present on the scene of the unrest, and a psychiatric counselor for undergraduates. He was able to combine his personal involvement with an academic-scientific orientation. He used psychological methods and studies of counselees to focus on a social pathology rather than solely on individual pathology. His personal frame of reference and its influence on his research were acknowledged, like Roger Kahn (1970); he does not offer his research as "unbiased." Like Kunen (1970) and Rosenkrantz (1971), he was sympathetic to the concerns and demands of the students. (However, unlike Kunen and Rosenkrantz, he was not a student.) Neither was he like R. Kahn, a professional writer. His orientation as a psychiatrist and concern as a counselor motivated him to examine how a socially pathological situation (the Vietnam War and Columbia's connection with the war effort) could influence certain students to react by sit-ins at Columbia.

In his interviews with students, Libert found from a social psychological perspective that the students were reacting and opposing certain movements they understood to be prevalent in society at large. Libert implied that there was a connection between the real social situation (United States at war in Vietnam) and the awareness of this situation (with accompanying resentment) by students opposed to the war. Additional awareness (by the demonstrators and those who became sympathetic toward them and offered support) came into being during the interaction of the students with a symbolic outside social agency (the police). Libert's interpretations were based upon his research into the social extrinsic factors and their influence upon the subjective or psychological value judgments of the demonstrators and their sympathizers.

*College—* Columbia University

*Title— University in Turmoil:*

*The Politics of Change*

*Author—* Immanuel Wallerstein

Wallerstein (1969) characterizes *University in Turmoil* as the "fruit of intensely experiencing the dramatic events that broke out at Columbia University on April 23, 1968, and that have not yet ended as of this writing" (p. vii). He distinguished between normal and abnormal functions of government and discussed the role of any university having a direct liaison with a government. In particular he concerned himself with such university/government liaison when the government is functioning in a way that is believed by a significant and vociferous minority to be abnormal. According to Wallerstein, students found Columbia to be involved with the U.S. government's actions in Vietnam, and opposed the university having a direct liaison with the government. According to Wallerstein, the students decided to bring political pressure on Columbia because of its connection with the government or certain social issues, e.g., Vietnam.

According to *University in Turmoil*, Wallerstein was an associate professor of sociology on the faculty at Columbia. He was also a member of the Columbia Ad Hoc Faculty Group, specifically the branch known as the Columbia Ad Hoc Steering Committee. This group had many diverse elements but were uniformly opposed to police intervention and sympathetic to student demands. Cox (1968) found that the Ad Hoc Faculty Group's (AHFG) actions did little more than polarize the situation and "the efforts of members of the faculty to resolve the crisis brought them into conflict with each other and with the administration" (p. 155). Wallerstein was also the original chairman of the Faculty Civil Rights Group (founded in 1966), and the first executive secretary of the Executive Committee on Faculty. As a member of these groups, he was involved in the 1968 Columbia events.

> These events forced me, as they did most persons caught up in them, to give more careful and concentrated consideration to questions that had long since been of concern. . . . History catches up with most of us and forces choices—political and moral—that we would not otherwise look forward to making. (p. vii)

Like Bennis (1973), Wallerstein was concerned with his role and also with his search for answers to the problem of student unrest. Wallerstein discussed "the issues that underlay the event [Columbia] and many other events that occurred last year" (p. viii).

Wallerstein wrote *University in Turmoil* in "an attempt to resist being overwhelmed by the day-by-day developments" (p. viii). He stated that his writing was the result of his personal involvement with the events that broke out in April, 1968 at Columbia. Although Wallerstein did not detail his involvement, based upon his membership in faculty groups that were concerned about police action, he was involved in what he described as intense and personal actions at the time of the Columbia demonstrations. According to Wallerstein, societal factors were a cause of student unrest. He stated repeatedly in *University in Turmoil* that the war in Vietnam and the problems of students with the draft were two general areas of social concern.

At Columbia, in addition to these general areas of social concern there were the issues of the involvement of Columbia with the Institute of Defense Analysis and the impact of the building of the gymnasium in the Harlem Community. Wallerstein, however, does not dwell on the events at Columbia, but these issues and events provided him with an opportunity or an occasion to show how social factors such as the Vietnam War could influence the function of a community. Wallerstein (1969) found that "the various instances of University turmoil are the consequences of social problems that are common to industrialized countries of the world" (p. viii).

His active interest in student and civil rights was indicated by his charter membership and first chairmanship of the Faculty Civil Rights Group. Wallerstein had been teaching at Columbia since 1958. At the time of the Columbia demonstrations, he was an associate professor of sociology. Based upon Wallerstein's comments in *University in Turmoil*, and his activities as member of faculty groups with liberal orientations, this writer concluded that Wallerstein viewed social causes as the most significant causes of student unrest. He saw the university as needing social change which continued unrest would bring about. Wallerstein predicted, "No doubt harassment will over time have the same effect on the university as it has on the general society . . . serious negotiations and concessions" (p. 124)

Wallerstein's leftist sympathies and his view of students revolting against society (Columbia being the symbol) were commented upon later in his book:

> As with most social conflicts, it is with the emergence of a vocal left movement among those with relatively few privileges in the system (in this case, the students) that the issues have become politically real. . . . This did not occur as an isolated phenomenon of the university. It came within and because of a particular series of developments in the *larger national society*. (p. 133) (Emphasis added.)

*Conclusion.* Wallerstein experienced student unrest and decided to review the goals and role of a university from a leftist frame of reference and with an assumption of a need for social change. Bennis (1973) had also written *The Leaning Ivory Tower* with the explicit intent of similar introspection, but his focus was on the institution and its implementation of policies rather than on the need for social change. However, both Bennis and Wallerstein experienced student unrest and decided to write on their role and goals. Wallerstein's focus as well as his style was also quite different than Libert's, although both were members of the faculty. Wallerstein, in spite of his involvement with the activists, chose to write with a view toward the future of the university, rather than toward the reaction of students to the same Columbia perspective. Both Libert and Wallerstein viewed society as the chief factor in student unrest, in spite of their differences regarding the context and purpose of their books reviewed in this section.

*College*— Kent State

*Title—Kent State: What Happened and Why*

*Author*— James A. Michener

> The root of the problem at Kent State was lack of communication. . . . With everyone shouting at one another, no one could be heard, until the forces

*Chapter III*

unleashed by official ineptitude, inflammatory political rhetoric, and arson crystallized into a burst of gunfire.... Such conduct set the stage for the biggest peaceful assembly in the history of Kent State University, a demonstration to protest not the war, not Cambodia, but the continued presence of the Ohio National Guard on Campus. (Davies et al., 1973, p. 28)

According to Michener, on April 30, 1970, President Richard Nixon announced that United States forces fighting in Vietnam would cross over into Cambodia to destroy enemy sanctuaries. Kent State students demonstrated against the Cambodian invasion and on May 2, the Reserve Officers Training Corps Building at Kent was set afire and burned to the ground. The Governor of Ohio, James A. Rhodes, sent the National Guard (approximately 750 guardsmen) to Kent, Ohio, to prevent civil disruptions throughout the city. On May 4, 1970, the guardsmen on campus at Kent State fired both tear gas and guns at the students. Four students were killed; nine were injured.

James Michener was the author of a day-by-day, hour-by-hour reconstruction and report of these events (May 1–May 4, 1970). He visited Kent State in the summer and fall of 1970 when the events were still fresh, still being reviewed, constantly discussed, and still had many ramifications, both social and emotional that were unsettled and in process.

In his reconstruction of the events, Michener explained that he attempted to recreate the events according to the recollection of those who could be interviewed and who were involved in some way. However as Michener stated, his visits to Kent State occurred during the summer and fall of 1970 and his reconstruction was therefore influenced by who was available for interview and by the discussions or "post mortems" probably conducted by those interviewed (National Guardsmen, students, etc.) who spoke to each other about these events.

Michener told of his presence at Kent State when the events and emotional climate were still immediate and proximate. His stringent descriptions, his minute-by-minute account of the three days of disorder (on and off campus) preceding the shootings were induced from interviews with eyewitnesses, students, faculty, college, state and local officials, radical leaders, policemen, bartenders, and parents. His material was further developed as he described and analyzed the issues and events as well as the activities (within that context) of the four students who were killed. When events were recalled in a manner that conflicted with other persons' recollections he presented both sides.

Per the definition given previously, societal (causes) pertained to social factors whose policies and substantive components originated off campus and were related to national and international situations. The National Guard was not requested by the college administrators to appear on an already volatile campus. Both the presence of the National Guard as well as the issues and some of the demonstrators were considered outside (or societal) causes by Michener. He commented on outside factors:

> Allan Orashan, the Sigma Alpha Epsilon Leader who spells Eddie Kaufman at J. B.'s door says, "I know the Water Street regulars. Friday night I saw half a dozen strangers who were giving the crowd direction. When the rock-throwing and window-smashing began, it was as much non-student as student." (p. 60)

Michener also told of four Weathermen in September, 1969, who had explained to a student that the Weathermen had decided to close down colleges across the United States. He said that it was clear by Friday, May 1, 1970, that "Kent State was a target of considerable outside interest and interest expressed through violence" (p. 61).

Michener felt that murder was not committed by the National Guard:

> It was an accident deplorable and tragic. If evidence should surface to prove there was collusion or that certain guardsmen boasted on Sunday night that "tomorrow I'm gonna shoot me some students," this conclusion would look ridiculous, but such evidence was not available to us, even though we searched for it most diligently. There was death, but not murder. (pp. 365–366)

Michener felt that the deaths and subsequent events on Kent State campus and colleges throughout the nation were caused by other additional factors outside the campus.

> We have been much impressed by the pastoral calm shown in photographs of the Commons taken before noon that day and have had to conclude that the students did not gather to riot . . . so it is logical to argue that had the guard not been there, *no disturbance would have developed.* (pp. 365–366) (Emphasis added.)

Although Michener found the presence of the National Guard inflammatory, he saw different societal factors than Wallerstein (1969). Wallerstein perceived the actions as caused by those who wanted social change and was sympathetic toward the ends and means of the demonstrators. Michener, however, was more defensive of the status quo and viewed confrontations more negatively than Wallerstein. In his conclusions, Michener deplored student demonstrations and found them to be caused by revolutionaries. Michener, based upon his research, concludes:

> Young people who brazenly defy soldiers, daring them to shoot, commit more than suicide; they commit a grave crime against organized society. . . . We were driven to one final and significant conclusion. The hard-core revolutionary leadership across the nation was so determined to force a confrontation—which would result in gunfire and the radicalization of the young—that some kind of

major incident had become inevitable.... That it happened at Kent State was
pure accident, but the confrontation itself was not. (pp. 367–368)

Michener was a professional writer commissioned by the *Reader's Digest* and students of Kent State School of Journalism. Michener described his background and methods as:

Swarthmore, 1929 and perpetually concerned about what young people are doing.... I slipped into a motel, spent a week walking around the city and reading back copies of *The Record-Courier* and *The Daily Kent Starter*, the University paper. I spent my nights in the bars on North Water Street sitting in a corner and listening. It was eight days before anyone knew what I was; by then I had a feel for Kent and had made a series of friendships which would continue throughtout my stay.... How did I work? I let it be known that I was eager to listen to anyone in Kent who had strong ideas about what had happened.... When a practiced writer does this quietly and with enough time so he is not hurried, he finds an amazing sequence of visitors coming to his door. (p. 511)

*Conclusion. Kent State: What Happened and Why* had as its central focus and as its climax the May 4 killings and the national ramifications. Michener found societal causes as the most significant factor in student unrest. Michener had graduated in 1929 from Swarthmore College, was a professional writer, and a thorough researcher. His interview techniques and general modus operandi resembled those of Roger Kahn (1970). The fact that he wrote for the conservative press, i.e., the *Reader's Digest*, may have influenced his conclusions drawn from his data, but such an association was not easily ascertainable from the information in the book. Michener seemed, as shown above, to be oriented towards a society (the United States) that he saw threatened by revolutionary social forces that sought confrontations with the authorities. Michener's frame of reference was the maintenance of our society, and he did not as Wallerstein (1969) address the concept of social change. To Michener, the impingement of outside forces was negative and conclusive to social instability and radicalization.

*College—* Kent State

*Title— The Killings at Kent State: How Murder Went Unpunished*

*Author—* I. F. Stone

The title, *The Killings at Kent State: How Murder Went Unpunished* (1971), is indicative of I. F. Stone's findings regarding the events at Kent State. From his own review of the events and his research into documents included in his Appendix, Stone offered his analysis of events and concluded that the Guardsmen committed murder and that the subsequent Grand Jury Investigation Report was a whitewash based in part on insufficient data. He claimed the cause of the killings and subsequent unrest was the overreaction of fatigued National Guardsmen.

Stone visited the Kent State University Campus in the fall of 1970. He was sympathetic to the students:

> I spoke with as many students as I could in a two-day visit. By the time I left I had a real feeling of respect and affection for the youngsters I had met and I understood how rewarding they could seem to their best teachers.... Among those in the class (a class visited by Stone) were veterans of the Vietnam War radicalized by their experiences and frustrated by their parents' unwillingness to listen to them. (pp. 35–36)

In addition to his visit on campus, Stone examined and included in his work the FBI Reports and the Grand Jury Report. He was critical of the Scranton Report (President's Commission on Campus Unrest, 1970) also known as *The Report of the President's Commission on Campus Unrest.* According to Stone, it did not go far enough and "the destructive potential ... comes from the fact that they have honestly and thoroughly shown that the killings were unjustified and unnecessary," yet, "do not put the spotlight on those responsible for the killings" (pp. 15–16)

Although Stone was writing and researching in the fall of 1970, he did not visit the Kent State University Campus while the events were still recent or at a time when the reports mentioned above were currently being published. His writing and research were influenced by his methods of journalistic interview and data review plus his sympathetic interest in the students protesting against the incursion of United States troops into Cambodia.

Stone was a professional writer and wrote for his own liberally-oriented publication, *I. F. Stone's Weekly.* The focus of his book was on the killings and the legal and formal investigations that he felt covered up blame for the riots and killings. Stone was against the United States war in Cambodia and Vietnam.

It should be noted that Davies et al. (1973), in *The Truth About Kent State: A Challenge to the American Conscience,* reached conclusions very similar to those of Stone. Davies and the Board of Church and Society of the United Methodist Church researched and wrote *The Truth About Kent State.* The book was not included in the body of selected literature because it was neither a single author's work nor written during or immediately after the May 4, 1970 events at Kent State. However, the conclusions reached in this work are consistent (albeit based upon new evidence and data) with Stone's (1971) conclusions that societal factors, i.e., presence of the National Guard and their unwarranted actions, caused the student unrest on May 4, 1970, at Kent State. *The Truth About Kent State* was also consistent with Stone's claim of a whitewash by the Portage County (Ohio) Grand Jury Report which investigated these events at Kent State.

Davies was an insurance broker. He had sent a letter of protest to President Nixon and a copy to the father of Allison Krause, a woman who had been killed by a bullet fired by a National Guardsman on May 4, 1970 at Kent State University. *The Truth About Kent State* was later undertaken to urge further inquiry into possible explanations of the shootings based upon a review of the old evidence and upon the additional evidence. The purpose of this work was to establish that justice can only be served where there is a desire to serve it by considering all available data. Davies et al. maintained that no one should be above the law nor below it.

*Conclusion.* From Stone's perspective, he considered the causes to be social in origin. His research and analysis (including two days spent on the Kent State campus) about the killings led him to believe that there had been a coverup by the authorities. Hence, he saw an injustice in the murders which was complicated by a coverup effort by powers wishing to maintain or justify the killings as "unfortunate" without blaming anyone but the victims. Stone was also critical of Governor Rhodes' decision to call up guardsmen already fatigued from riot duty in Cleveland, Ohio.

This writer found Stone (1971) and Michener (1971) to be professional writers with different orientations. Stone was more liberal than Michener, found societal factors as the significant cause of the killings, and blamed the National Guard for murder. He also accused those having authority in the society beyond Kent State of a whitewash. As stated previously, Michener also found societal causes to be a significant factor in the killings and the general unrest preceding them. For Michener, however, these societal factors consisted of outside forces trying to radicalize students. He was not in favor of such radicalizing and did not find a whitewash being attempted.

*College*—California State College, San Francisco

*Title*—*Blow It Up: The Black Student Revolt at San Francisco State College and the Emergence of Dr. Hayakawa*

*Author*—Dikran Karagueuzian

According to *Blow It Up: The Black Student Revolt at San Francisco State College and the Emergence of Dr. Hayakawa* (1971), Dikran Karagueuzian was a former editor of the campus publication, *The San Francisco State Gator*. He explained that during what he called the Black Students Union strike at State College of California, San Francisco he was on the scene and doing journalistic studies of the events. Karagueuzian gave character sketches of the participants and discussed general causes and issues of the strike. The issues he cited were similar to those delineated by Boyle (1970).

The Black Students Union supported the black students and demanded an autonomous (i.e., free from interference by the college or trustees) black studies department having 20 full-time black faculty. Other issues were open admissions for all black applying for admission in 1969 and the reinstatement of George Mason Murray as part-time English instructor. Murray was the Black Panther Minister of Education and had encouraged black students to carry guns for protection against racists.

Karagueuzian's book was a day-to-day account of the strike with focus on the chronological developments and specifically on how the black and white radical leaders worked together. Karagueuzian maintained that due to the issues and the cohesiveness of the radical groups, these groups had more influence than the black and white moderates.

Karagueuzian was more interested in reporting than in analysis. He attempted journalistic objectivity and, therefore, offered little analysis. Although it has been stated that the issues he cited were similar to Boyle's, Karagueuzian gives more emphasis to the black student movement. His reportage gave more attention to the sympathy of other radical movements and to the societal significance of black student protest in general rather than to institutional factors.

Journals and character sketches were two of the methods used by selected authors to record the events of student unrest. When these methods were used by Dikran Karagueuzian, the focus as aforementioned was on the day-do-day events and current implications, and little information was provided concerning his stance regarding the issues or his orientation. However, it may be induced that, according to how he reported the events (i.e., relating them to a social movement and showing how radicals on campus could work together in bringing about positive change for black students), Karagueuzian was sympathetic to the black student demands. Certainly, his orientation as editor of *The San Francisco State Gator* had given him knowledge of the situation at San Francisco State College—at least from a student reporter perspective: "The student newspaper, the *Daily Gator*, [was] . . . a strong supporter

*Chapter III*

of the strike.... The administration has insisted that the *Gator* coverage of the strike has often been unreliable" (Orrick, 1969, p.46).

*Conclusion.* Karagueuzian was an editor of a student daily newspaper that supported the strike. He endeavored in his day-do-day reporting to show the cohesiveness of the Black Student Union and radical white support groups. Little attempt was made at analysis for the thrust of the book is historical and concerned with the strike's macrocosmic and social significance. Based upon available data in this book for analysis, we are able to induce that an editor (Karagueuzian) for a student newspaper sympathetic to a student strike wrote a day-to-day journal covering the strike. This editor attempted little analysis in his reportage but emphasized the issues as being societal in their causes. He also emphasized that the cooperation of black and white radical groups was also socially significant.

*College*—California State College, San Francisco

*Title*—*Shut It Down! A College in Crisis, San Francisco State College, October, 1968–April, 1969*

*Author*—William H. Orrick, Jr.

William H. Orrick, Jr. was the author of a staff report to the National Commission on the Causes and Prevention of Violence completed in 1969. *Shut It Down! A College in Crisis* is, according to Orrick, a report that "draws no conclusions from the tragic events that overtook San Francisco State in the fall and winter of 1968–1969," even though it was the product of "many days . . . spent on the campus viewing the actual physical confrontation" (p. ix). Orrick described some of the violent events that occurred during the strike:

> On November 6, the black students finding their demands unmet launched a strike against San Francisco State College. A week later, 65 faculty members joined the students on the picket lines.
>
> In the following weeks, San Francisco State College was the scene of violence unmatched in the history of American higher education. The campus became the first to be occupied by police on a continuous basis over several months, and it was only the daily presence of 200 to 600 policemen which kept the college open....
>
> By the end of the semester on January 31, 1969, there had been 731 arrests on campus, more than 80 students were reported injured as they were arrested, and others were hurt and not arrested. Thirty-two policemen were injured on the campus. Damage to campus buildings exceeded $16,000; there were scores of

small fires and a major one in a vice president's office. Eight bombs were planted on campus, and two firebombs were hurled at and into the home of an assistant to the President. In mid-February, a campus guard received head injuries from a bomb that exploded at the entrance to the administration building. Three weeks later, on March 5, 1969 a 19-year-old Negro sophomore in social sciences was partially blinded and maimed when a time bomb—which police said he was installing—exploded in the Creative Arts Building. (Orrick, 1969, pp. 2–4)

Orrick then explained the purpose and plan of his book:

Why, then, did the San Francisco State College strike become the first sustained assault on an institution . . . ? . . . This report addresses itself to answering this question, and in so doing provides insights into some of the causes. . . . It focuses on the underlying reasons for the strike . . . it presents, as objectively as possible, the attitudes of representatives of the various groups which were embroiled in the controversy. (p. 4)

Orrick and his team concluded 400 individual interviews and studied 1,200 newspaper articles. He received cooperation from the governor of California, mayor of San Francisco, F.B.I., San Francisco Police Department, Chancellor of California State Colleges, trustees of California State College, acting President (Hayakawa) of San Francisco State College, dean, faculty, legislators, public officials, and many student leaders (Orrick, p. ix). Orrick did not identify such student leaders or their organizations so there is some question regarding how much cooperation was extended by the Black Students Union and the Third World Liberation Front.

Orrick (1969), Boyle (1970), and Karagueuzian (1971) agreed on the issues being the demands of the Black Students Union and the demands of the Third World Liberation Front.

As mentioned previously, Orrick was a professional researcher for the National Commission on the Causes and Prevention of Violence. He was on the scene and worked with a team of researchers during and after the events. Orrick saw the causes of student unrest as transcending the issues. In other words, he considered the issues to be symptomatic of the real causes. Although he states that the "report draws no conclusions from the tragic events that overtook San Francisco State" (Orrick, p. ix), he does comment on the causes as

deeply rooted problems which . . . remain to be solved. Among these problems are longstanding social and economic injustices and inequities and the reluctance of the

*Chapter III*  74

so called establishment to respond rapidly to the need for change. (p. 147)

Orrick also saw the causes as societal in that the strike reflected the "economic and social imbalances which bitterly divide the American people today" (p. 147). The issues were symptomatic of a New Left movement that, according to Orrick, "seeks ... the destruction of higher education and its visible institutions as they are presently constituted" (p. 148). Orrick is included in the category of professional writer although he could be considered the least published of these authors under this category. He was not a student, a college faculty member, nor a college administrator. He is included in the category of professional writers because as a professional researcher and director of a study team, part of his task was to write such reports. In turn these reports were published and subject to the same scrutiny as the works of other authors. According to Dr. Milton S. Eisenhower, Chairman of the National Commission on the Causes and Prevention of Violence:

> Both the credit and the responsibility for the reports lie in each case with the directors of the task forces and study teams. The Commission is making the reports available at this time as works of scholarship to be judged on their merits, so that the Commission as well as the public may have the benefit of both the reports and informed criticism and comment on their contents. (Orrick, p. iii)

*Conclusion.* Orrick, as a member of "the establishment" Commission criticized by the New Left, viewed with alarm any change based upon violence and destruction of our social system. He found the causes to be societal for two reasons. They were: (1) the social/economic problems of our society as reflected in our institutions of higher learning such as San Francisco State; (2) the existence of New Left groups whose remedy to those problems is based upon violence rather than working within the system.

Orrick's stand is based upon the concept of working for improvement by reforming rather than destroying the system. He cited issues and related them to the need for social change. His concern is that if the social problems are not remedied by the establishment, then the problems will cause violent endeavors to be extended against the establishment.

Orrick had focused upon the concept as he perceived it of social ills causing radical change. Karagueuzian, however, viewed the unrest at San Francisco State as one way in which radical groups can affect change. Boyle, also writing about San Francisco State, saw the unrest as caused by institutional incompetence and did not address the larger social factors cited by Orrick and Karagueuzian.

*College*—Yale

*Title*—*Letter to the Alumni*

*Author*—John Hersey

The above book has already been discussed under a section of this chapter titled "Institutional Causes." The events at May Day 1970, the issues, and the author's orientation have already been reviewed. As it has been shown, Hersey (1970) credited Yale President Kingman Brewster with having been tuned into the feelings of both the Yale community and the New Haven community at large. Hersey credited Brewster's perception of the mood on campus and the administration's decision to have classes made optional during the May 1970 events with keeping Yale from having a greater degree of student unrest. In other words these institutional factors had been offered by Hersey as determining the type of student unrest (limited and without confrontation and violence seen in other demonstrations at Yale). Since *Letter to the Alumni* was the only book to have such a thrust, this writer viewed the institution, as shown by Hersey, as causing this particular form of unrest.

However, Hersey also described the concern of the Yale community and the New Haven black community over the two Black Panthers pending trial for murder. Both communities were concerned that the Black Panthers could not, perhaps, get a fair trial. Such concerns had been the *origin* of the events, but the form of the events was controlled by the institution.

*Conclusion.* Hersey was a professional writer concerned with social concerns. He was a liberal and had written this book for a traditional audience (Yale alumni). He was an administrator at Yale and as such had an interest in a Yale that was viable and not destroyed by outside forces. This stance was expanded by many indications that Hersey was critical of our society but did not want it destroyed but changed from within. His concern for such change was manifested in his praise of the institution for accommodating a controlled May Day. He, therefore, saw society responsible for the substance of the May Day demonstration and viewed the institution as responsible for the form and type of demonstration.

*College*— Yale

*Title*—*May Day at Yale: A Case Study in Student Radicalism*

*Author*—John Taft

Taft was a Yale undergraduate during 1970. Although his book, *May Day at Yale:*

Chapter III  76

*A Case Study in Student Radicalism*, was written in 1976 and included hindsight-type interviews with Kingman Brewster in 1972, it was based on his observations and actions during late April and May 1970 at which time Taft was, according to his account, both on the scene and involved. In other words, Taft based his findings on the events of 1970 and not their results or ramifications. His conclusion was that societal factors such as the pending trial and Yale's concern about the black community were the causes of the May Day events.

According to Taft Yale's campus community became politically conscious in the spring of 1970 when Erica Huggins and Bobby Seale, members of the Black Panther Party, went on trial for murder. Alleged police harassment of the Black Panthers, the style of the Black Panthers, and the awareness of the plight of the New Haven black community all had an effect on the Yale community, causing it (or community members) to take cognizance of a social situation. There now existed on Yale's campus a desire for Yale to do something for the local black community. Taft described the interaction and dialogue between diverse groups from university and community factions and reported that it was agreed that there would be an optional suspension of classes and a rally held on May 1.

Taft offered his personal observations of the May Day event and described Yale's ambivalence over the scholarship and activist roles of a university. Taft stated that the students were influenced by nonacademic and political events and described the strike as an irrational attempt by white students to ease feelings of shame regarding the black situation in New Haven.

The Yale community experienced an impingement from the society outside of Yale. This impingement took the form of a growing awareness and concern about the New Haven black community precipitated by the Black Panther trial. Taft found the strike to be a symbolic apology of Yale for the way things were in society—actually right in New Haven.

Taft gives little information about himself other than that he was a student in his 20s and was on campus during the May Day events. Like Kelman (1970), Taft was critical of the type of student unrest, claiming it was based on guilt feelings rather than the original issues. Unlike Wallerstein (1969), he does not see the university as having an active role in social change citing the ineffectiveness of a strike as a means of improving things.

*Conclusion.* Perhaps it was the time lapse (this book was published at a date later than all of the others), but the style and content of May Day at Yale tell us very little about Taft. In attempting to ascertain knowledge of an author's background, this writer found insufficient data for any further comments except to say that this book demonstrated great objectivity.

Regardless of whether or not the authors so far examined in this section agreed, disagreed, or gave little or ample indication of their personal feelings regarding the issues, all concluded that the causes of unrest had origin not with the student or the college but with macro-societal factors.

*College*—Northwestern University

*Title—Student Protest and the Technocratic Society: The Case of ROTC*

*Author*—Jack Nusan Porter

According to Porter (1973) he revised his Ph.D. (Sociology, Northwestern University) dissertation and published it as *Student Protest and the Technocratic Society: The Case of ROTC* (1973). In this revised dissertation, Porter gave a general background of the student unrest leading up to the damage to the Reserve Officers Training Corps Building at Northwestern University. Porter reported that in May 1970, 100 students demonstrated and caused damage to the ROTC Building. Of the 100 students who participated 45 were arrested.

Porter was a graduate student in sociology at the time. He began his research and data gathering/analysis immediately after the demonstration damage and arrests.

Porter perceived the university as a microcosm of our growing technocratic society and ROTC as an ostensible issue. Porter believed that opposition to ROTC was in fact opposition to the social canonization of specialized techniques at the cost of humanistic individualistic concerns. Porter saw the university as "linked into the military-industrial complex that lies at the foundation of technocratic society"(p. 5), and perceived the student unrest as caused by student opposition to unwanted social forces impinging upon the university.

This unwanted social force at Northwestern was, according to Porter, the Reserve Officers Training Corps (ROTC) which served as a symbol of the technocratic society. Porter sought to explain the causes of student unrest in social, rather than psychological terms, and proposed that such unrest should be seen as a response to concrete societal pressure such as the Vietnam War.

Porter's views are similar to those of Menhart (1976) who described student anxiety related to the technocratic age.

> Many students fear that someday they may be superfluous because there might

not be enough jobs for the armies of university graduates. If they study liberal arts, they are apprehensive that, in what Zbigniev Brzezinski, formerly of Columbia University, called the technotronic age that they will be outdated, discarded, shunted off.... Since nothing creates closer ties than facing the same enemy, many prefer groups which stand in opposition to society. (p. 347)

Porter claimed that:

To view student protest as a response to technocratic pressures raises our horizons by merging the individual, his society, and his historical setting. Social scientists have too often concentrated on the psychological and the parental reasons for student protest, and have avoided intensively analyzing, or even mentioning, the technocratic. (p. 5)

As a graduate student in sociology, Porter shared in an interest and an evaluation (both positive and negative) of the technocratic theories. Porter's position may be best revealed by his dissertation in sociology which focuses on the ROTC as an indication of technocratic emphasis in the society. He was on the scene at the time of the unrest at Northwestern and was actively involved in gathering data for his Ph.D. dissertation. The situation provided Porter with an opportunity to exercise his frame of reference and to apply the technocratic theory model to the unrest found on the campus of Northwestern.

*Conclusion.* Porter found that student concerns about social issues caused students to demonstrate. The ROTC Building symbolized a social force which the students opposed in its connection with the draft and the Vietnam War. Hence Porter found the damage to the ROTC Building to be symbolic of the reaction of 100 students to social pressures. He does not address himself to the fact that 100 students at Northwestern were certainly a minority. His main thesis was that student unrest should be examined from a perspective that has as its base the question of how social force (e.g., Vietnam War, draft) influences student unrest.

## SUMMARY

The selected authors in this section found that student unrest was symptomatic of our society's ills. Hersey, Karagueuzian, Michener, Orrick, and Stone had had professional writing experience. Hersey, Michener, and Stone had a journalistic background, Orrick was a technical reporter, and Karagueuzian was both student and journalist. All of these authors viewed student unrest as a microcosm of social ills, and as such, related student unrest to social factors transcending the institutional and socialization concerns found in other literature on student unrest. Libert (1971), Porter (1973), Taft (1976), and Wallerstein (1969) were more oriented (as students or faculty) toward the institution than the professional writers. Their focus was on the agents of student unrest, i.e., students, professors, and administrators, involved in the subculture of the university.

Although Trilling (1978) was critical of the methods and substance of the student unrest at Columbia, she cited social factors as the causes and commented that institutional policies were of secondary importance to activist leaders:

> The uprising had the declared intention of large *social destructiveness* [emphasis added], the largest. In an open letter to President Grayson Kirk on April 22, Mark Rudd wrote: "We will destroy your university, your world, your corporation, your university.". . . Of course, so extreme an intention didn't motivate everyone who took part in the occupation. But the uprising is not properly understood unless this avowed goal of its leadership is held firmly to view. (Trilling, 1978, pp. 101–102)

> The phenomenon being reported on was not of the gutter. This violence and nastiness took place at an Ivy League university. The speech and acts which our newspapers and television withheld from the public were the speech and acts of young people who supposedly represent the American educated middle classes in their *most ardent desire to rid us of the indecencies of our present society* [emphasis added], and one discovered that a decent proportion of the decent American middle-calss mothers and fathers of these young people, as well as other energetic spokesmen for progress, supported their offspring. (Trilling, 1978, pp. 113–114)

She also found this wish to destroy our social system in the goals of the SDS.

As stated previously, all of the authors included in this section found social ills as a causal factor in student unrest. Hersey (1970) was specific in his focus on problems of the black community. Karagueuzian (1971) and Wallerstein (1969) were in agreement about the issues transcending university policies. Michener (1971), Stone (1971), and Orrick (1969) reported with different emphases and for diffferent reasons.

The selected literature presented in this chapter has been analyzed according to the methods adopted by this study as described in Chapter II. The data were categorized according to the type of cause (institution, socialization, or societal) given exclusive or emphatic consideration by the selected authors, and the authors' frames of references were scrutinized. As an alternative the selected literature could have been

## TABLE 2
### INSTITUTIONS DISCUSSED IN CHAPTER III BY FOUR OR MORE AUTHORS

| Name of Author | College Discussed by Author as a Scene of Student Unrest — Harvard | Columbia | Type of Cause Emphasized by Author — Institutional | Sociali-zation | Societal | Author's Background Given in Selected Literature — Faculty | Student | Professional Writer |
|---|---|---|---|---|---|---|---|---|
| A. Ulam | X | - | X | - | - | X | - | - |
| R. Zorza | X | - | X | - | - | - | X | - |
| S. Kelman | X | - | - | X | - | - | X | - |
| E. J. Kahn | X | - | - | X | - | - | - | X |
| R. Kahn | - | X | X | - | - | - | - | X |
| J. S. Kunen | - | X | X | - | - | - | X | - |
| R. Rosenkrantz | - | X | X | - | - | - | X | - |
| R. Libert | - | X | - | - | X | X | - | - |
| J. Wallerstein | - | X | - | - | X | X | - | - |

categorized according to institutions. However, since only Harvard and Columbia had a sampling of more than three authors such a categorization would not offer an appropriate or sufficient comparative scheme of analysis. However, in the cases of Harvard and Columbia such an alternative analysis is feasible. It is offered here as another dimension in the review of the literature, specifically, a cross analysis of the categories of causes. The findings of this analysis are illustrated in Table 2.

Harvard was discussed by four authors in particular, Ulam (1972), Zorza (1970), Kelman (1970), and E. J. Kahn, Jr. (1969). None of these authors, regardless of his background, mentioned or emphasized societal factors as a chief cause of student unrest. Ulam (1972), a faculty member criticized the Harvard administration for not minding its own business. He found that the actions of the Harvard administration caused both the climate and the actual events of unrest at Harvard. Zorza (1970) was also critical of the Harvard administration but for different reasons than those given by Ulam. While Ulam criticized the institutional policies as going too far, Zorza thought that the administration did not go far enough in listening to the students' concerns. It should be noted that Ulam was a tenured professor and Zorza was a student, who as he stated, had come from England and was in America three years and at Harvard two years when the unrest occurred. To summarize, Zorza and Ulam were different in age, orientation, and differed on their perceptions of the institution's role in pursuing nonacademic concerns.

Kelman (1970) was also a student and shared Zorza's interest in leftist views and his belief that Harvard should be more involved in student concerns. Kelman felt that the apathy and myopic vision of the Harvard administrators provided a minority of the students with the opportunity for the demonstration, but stressed the socialization of the students as the real cause of the particular type of unrest. E. J. Kahn, Jr. (1969) who was a professional writer and a graduate of Harvard similarly found that student socialization was the main cause of unrest.

When comparing all four authors, no concrete association can be found connecting their views and their backgrounds. The only commonalities are an absence of attention to societal causes and an emphasis upon institutional and socialization factors. Emphasis upon either of these latter two was not related to the author's age. Despite their age differences both Ulam and Zorza stressed institutional causes; while both E. J. Kahn and Kelman who were also of different ages stressed socialization causes.

None of the five authors who wrote about Columbia emphasized socialization

*Chapter III*

factors. Three of the five (Kahn, Kunen, and Rosenkrantz) did emphasize institutional factors. R. Kahn (1970) who was a professional writer, and J.S. Kunen (1970) and R. Rosenkrantz (1971) who were students all described their participation in occupying campus buildings. Furthermore, all three were critical of the role of Columbia's administration and its institutional policies. Libert (1971) and Wallerstein (1969) were both members of the Columbia faculty and both focused on societal factors such as the Vietnam War and Columbia's involvement in war research as the cause of unrest. While Libert was concerned about the effects of unrest on students from a social psychological perspective, Wallerstein was concerned with the causes of unrest in general. However, both of these authors repeatedly referred to the larger social issues as the chief cause of unrest. Of the total of nine authors discussed, a majority of five cited institutitonal factors as the chief cause of unrest. Of the total of nine authors discussed, a majority of five cited institutional factors as the chief cause of student unrest. This majority of authors included two from Harvard and three from Columbia. Such emphasis on institutional factors transcended both the particular university and author background in that this view was shared among authors who were faculty, professional writers, and students at both Harvard and Columbia.

# IV
# SUMMARY, INTERPRETATION, AND CONCLUSION

We must love them both, those whose opinion we share and those whose opinions we reject. For both have labored in the search for truth and both have helped us in the finding of it. (St. Thomas Acquinas in T. Merton, 1966, p. 115)

## SUMMARY

This study was a critical review of the selected literature on college student unrest in the United States from 1968 to 1970. During this period, student unrest increased in both volume and violence. The purpose of this study was to:

1. Select a certain body of significant literature.
2. Review and analyze the literature to ascertain how the authors explained causes of student unrest.
3. Examine these explanations and also any available information about the authors as induced from the literature.
4. Determine if the authors' experiences and frames of reference pertaining to student unrest reflected their explanations and influenced their views, and if so, to what degree.

The selected literature, as well as other student unrest literature, had not yet been reviewed as proposed by the writer (re: content and method). The causes, statistical

Chapter IV

occurrence, and a broad overview of the existing knowledge of student unrest was delineated in Chapter I. Examples of bibliographies and research findings were also provided to indicate the availability and diverse nature of theories of student unrest.

Also included in this study was a development of how the sociology of knowledge could be conceptualized as methodology for a review of the literature. As a method, the sociology of knowledge concerned itself with how the selected authors' perceptions and interpretations of student unrest are influenced by their possible biases or orientations, insofar as they could be induced from the selected literature.

The investigatory procedure was influenced by the technique of ascertaining the role of the authors' frames of reference as they viewed the causes of student unrest. The literature was selected in the following manner:

1. The literature would be in book form.
2. The book would have a single author.
3. The author would have been an observer or someway directly involved, or on a campus while the climate of student unrest was still existent.
4. The date of publication would be as proximate to the event as possible.

Both the causes and their categorization were induced from the selected literature. Ascertaining authors' orientations (or frames of reference) was done by analysis and implicit indications. The categories were gleaned and abstracted from the causes given by the authors. From the readings, it was determined what cause or causes (albeit not necessarily mutually exclusive of other causes) were given the most weight by the authors.

The research procedures produced a body of literature of 20 authors and the same number of books. The notions of causation were developed from the literature and evolved in three broad categories of causes. They were Institutional, Socialization, and Societal. Since, for example, (re: Socialization Causes) the intergenerational continuity and intergenerational conflict theories were not necessarily opposite theories, both positive and negative perspectives were included when appropriate within the same category.

According to the selected literature, the 20 authors wrote on nine different institutions. This is illustrated by Table 3.

As gleaned from the literature, only broad and somewhat vague orientations of the authors could be ascertained. This was a disappointment. It was anticipated that the approach used would have led to more insightful perceptions about the authors than

## TABLE 3
## INSTITUTIONS SELECTED BY THE AUTHORS REVIEWED IN CHAPTER III

| INSTITUTION | AUTHORS |
|---|---|
| 1. California State College at Fullerton | Epstein, Cy |
| 2. California State College at San Francisco | Boyle, Kay |
| | Karagueuzian, Dikran |
| | Orrick, William H., Jr. |
| 3. Columbia | Kahn, Roger |
| | Kunen, James Simon |
| | Libert, Robert |
| | Rosenkrantz, Richard |
| | Wallerstein, Immanuel |
| 4. Harvard | Kahn, E. J., Jr. |
| | Kelman, Steven |
| | Ulam, Adam |
| | Zorza, Richard. |
| 5. Kent State | Michener, James A. |
| | Stone, I. F. |
| 6. Northwestern | Porter, Jack Nusan |
| 7. State University of New York at Buffalo | Bennis, Warren G. |
| 8. University of California at Berkeley | Coyne, John R. |
| 9. Yale | Hersey, John |
| | Taft, John |

in fact occurred. Specifically it was expected that the authors would reveal more of their "background" and provide some basis for whatever selective perception was to be found. This analysis did not yield much of this material. Whether this shortcoming was due to the nature of the literature under analysis, the ability of the author or some other factors cannot be determined within this study. The authors, as it developed, fell into three broad categories. They were students, faculty or administration, and professional writers. (Some could fit into more than one category; e.g., Kay Boyle, a professional writer who was on the San Francisco State faculty.)

Table 4 illustrates and summarizes the selected literature in terms of the name of the author, type of author, categories of causes, and the name of the institution.

## INTERPRETATION

There were eight student authors, three citing societal, three institutional, and two socialization factors as causes of student unrest.

## TABLE 4
## SUMMARY OF ANALYSES OF AUTHORS USED IN THE REVIEW OF SELECTED LITERATURE, CHAPTER III

| Author | Type of Author[a] | Categories of Causes | Institution |
| --- | --- | --- | --- |
| Bennis, Warren G. | F/A | Institutional | SUNY, Buffalo |
| Boyle, Kay | PW | Institutional | California State College, Fullerton |
| Coyne, John R. | S | Socialization | University of California, Berkeley |
| Epstein, Cy | F | Institutional | California State College, San Francisco |
| Hersey, John | PW | Institutional/Societal | Yale |
| Kahn, E. J., Jr. | PW | Socialization | Harvard |
| Kahn, Roger | PW | Institutional | Columbia |
| Karagueuzian, Dikran | S | Societal | California State College, San Francisco |
| Kelman, Steven | S | Socialization | Harvard |
| Kunen, James Simon | S | Institutional | Columbia |
| Libert, Robert | F | Societal | Columbia |
| Michener, James A. | PW | Societal | Kent State |
| Orrick, William H., Jr. | PW | Societal | California State College, San Francisco |
| Porter, Jack Nusan | S | Societal | Northwestern |
| Rosenkrantz, Richard | S | Institutional | Columbia |
| Stone, I. F. | PW | Societal | Kent State |
| Taft, John | S | Societal | Yale |
| Ulam, Adam | F | Institutional | Harvard |
| Wallerstein, Immanuel | F | Societal | Columbia |
| Zorza, Richard | S | Institutional | Harvard |

[a] A = administrator; F = faculty; PW = professional writer; S = Student.

*Chapter IV*

The seven professional writers gave societal as a cause four times, institutional three times (one author was used twice), and socialization was given once.

Of the five remaining authors, four were faculty and one was an administrator. Three cited institutional causes and two cited societal.

The causes were cited in total as nine societal and nine institutional. Socialization was cited three times.

The above is an analysis of summary data given in Table 4 and is illustrated in Table 5.

The samplings, although extensive, limited this writer to the examination of certain variables. This was especially true when an attempt was made to view author type and causes from a third dimension—namely, the type of institution about which they wrote. Only Columbia, Harvard, and San Francisco State had three or more authors that discussed them in the selected literature.

Columbia and Harvard, for example, are considered Ivy League, prestigious institutions. San Francisco State is an example of a large state institution and less selective than Ivy League schools in terms of admission.

Tables 5 illustrates that both type schools, regardless of author type, gave predominance to the institutional and societal causes. Nine of the three authors from San Francisco State cited socialization, while only two of the nine authors from Ivy League schools (both from Harvard—one a professional writer and the other a student) cited socialization.

Another question raised by analysis of the selected literature was the possible association between the type of institution and the categories of causes and authors. As illustrated in Table 6, it is again found that there is no clear pattern of association between the variables. It is again found that there is a tendency for authors to cite societal and institutional factors as causes regardless of author and institutional typology. This is reinforced by Table 7 where all institutions, irrespective of the number of authors that discussed them in the selected literature were analyzed for possible relationships and patterns.

## CONCLUSION

In any analysis of data, consideration is given to determine if there are any significant meanings to the patterns or the lack of patterns. According to the selected literature analyzed in this chapter, relationships between the categories of authors and

Chapter IV

**TABLE 5**
**CATEGORIES OF CAUSES OF STUDENT UNREST FROM SELECTED LITERATURE AUTHORS AND AUTHOR TYPE**

| Type Author of Selected Literature | Socialization | Cause Institutional | Societal |
|---|---|---|---|
| Professional Writer | 1 | 3[a] | 4[a] |
| Student | 2 | 3 | 3 |
| Faculty/Administration | 0 | 3 | 2 |

[a]Same author (Hersey) used twice.

categories of causes, institutions and categories of causes, categories of authors and institutions there is no significant relationship. However, a preponderance of authors, transcending the categories of authors, gave predominance to both institutional and societal factors as causes of student unrest, giving socializational factors very little if any significance as causes.

This evidence leads to a rejection of the contention that the causes of student unrest as perceived by authors discussed in Chapter III could be explained simply by the author's orientations induced solely from this literature. However, within the context of this same methodology and data, it is interesting that societal and institutional factors (and not socialization) are perceived as causes by a majority (17 out of 20) of authors. As previously stated, these two factors transcended author typology. The analysis does not reveal much about the process used by the author in arriving at the causes.

Even though the social origins and validity of explanations of student unrest were not the objects of this paper, nevertheless certain tentative conclusions may be drawn, subject to further research. One obvious conclusion is that there are many theories of social phenomena and on what actually happened. The prevailing roles of an institution of higher learning made it quite vulnerable to activist demonstrations. Conversely, the prevailing roles of the students made them quite vulnerable to technological factors resulting in their feelings of alienation, impersonal bureaucratization, and the draft.

The categories of institutional causes, socialization causes, and societal causes included authors who were both critical or sympathetic to the activists. Hence, these categories provided a model to examine both positive and negative factors that pertained to notions of each of the causes. For example, an institution could be viewed as causing student unrest because of its policies. In turn, the policies could be viewed as causing the student unrest because they were either too sympathetic to students or had too little sympathy for their concerns.

All of the explanations given are plausible and consistent with the evidence cited by the authors. This may stem from the author's general bias toward a "cause" and selecting data to support that bias. There are also serious questions as to whether the data as presented is actual "evidence" of a cause and/or a serious test of alternate ideas about causes. That is, the "evidence" is not such that it supports only one of the "explanations." It does seem reasonable to suggest that the books analyzed should be viewed skeptically when taken as explanations of student unrest. This review reinforces the position that there are many facets of the same truth and no one perspective is all inclusive but rather a view of part of the truth.

TABLE 6
INSTITUTIONS THAT PERTAINED TO THREE OR MORE AUTHORS OF SELECTED LITERATURE AND CATEGORIES OF CAUSES AND AUTHOR TYPE

| Type Author of Selected Literature | Cause Socialization | Institutional | Societal |
|---|---|---|---|
| Professional Writer | Harvard[a] | Columbia[a] San Francisco[b] | San Francisco[b] |
| Student | Harvard[a] | Harvard[a] | San Francisco[b] Columbia[a] Columbia[a] |
| Faculty/Administrator | 0 | Harvard[a] | Columbia[a] Columbia[a] |

[a] Ivy League
[b] State College.

TABLE 7
INSTITUTIONS DISCUSSED BY AUTHORS OF SELECTED LITERATURE AND CATEGORIES OF CAUSES AND AUTHOR TYPE

| Type Author of Selected Literature | Socialization | Cause Institutional | Societal |
|---|---|---|---|
| Professional Writer | Harvard | Yale San Francisco Columbia | San Francisco Kent State Yale[a] |
| Student | Harvard Berkeley | Harvard Columbia Columbia | Northwestern Yale[a] San Francisco |
| Faculty/Administrator | 0 | Buffalo Fullerton Harvard | Columbia Columbia |

[a] Same author (Hersey) used twice.

# V
# IMPLICATIONS FOR FURTHER RESEARCH

> I should also point out that student protest does not occur in a vacuum, but is part—perhaps one of the most visible parts—of a deep and growing social unrest affecting much of the world. (Hitch, 1969)

Gwynn Nettler (1945) maintained that there are three factors to be considered when the sociology of knowledge is used to assess the author's perception of an event. They are (a) the social position of the author, (b) the type of event and how it relates to the social position of the author, and (c) the time at which the author has done his research and writing. Such a "test" could be applied to the data presented in this study and then expanded from the model of this study to include additional relevant data.

This study utilized parts of this approach in analyzing explanations of student unrest. The issues raised by this research probably overshadow any issues resolved by the current analysis.

There is no question that social phenomenon such as student unrest should be examined carefully and seriously. The current analysis seems to suggest that more carefully done analysis stemming from more varied and theoretical perspectives are in order. In turn, careful attention must be given to the form and source of data that will be accepted as testing these alternative hypotheses.

*Chapter V*

The sociology of knowledge perspective has proved useful in the current analysis in suggesting possible biases or other limitations in explanations given. Further research could profit from this healthy skepticism and the methodological implications it contains. This approach could also be used to view diverse elements of social life.

This study attempted to employ the sociology of knowledge as a basis for a method for determining how one's orientational frame of reference, as influenced by his socialization and social conditions, affects his perceptions and interpretations of social events. Nevertheless, the sociology of knowledge, as described by Nettler (1945), could not be sufficiently applied owing to the fact that there were only limited data available to this writer within the scope of his research to identify adequately the selected authors' orientational frame of reference. This larger analysis would require an extensive study of each author's life history bearing upon his interpretations of social events. Beyond the parameters of this study, a more elaborate relationship of factors among authors' orientations, causes of events and institutional types could be analyzed by incorporating additional data. This may be implemented by the use of this model as the initial phase in any such study.

The results obtained suggest that student unrest could profitably be reviewed using the perspectives adapted in this study.

# BIBLIOGRAPHY

I lay siege to truth . . . , first from one quarter and then another, expecting the reality to be not simpler than my experience of it, but far more extensive and complex. I stand in philosophy exactly where I stand in daily life. I should not be honest otherwise. I accept the same miscellaneous witness, bow to the same obvious facts, make conjectures no less instinctively, and admit the same encircling ignorance. (George Santayana in Stanford, 1964, p. i)

Adelson, J. Looking back. *Daedalus—American education: Toward an uncertain future,* Vol. I, Fall 1974, *103* (4), 54–57.

Altbach, P. G. *Student politics and higher education in the United States: A selected bibliography.* Introduction by S. M. Lipset. Cambridge, Mass.: Harvard Center for International Affairs, 1968.

Altbach, P. G., & Kelly, D. H. *American students: A selected bibliography on student activism and related topics.* Lexington, Mass.: Lexington Books, 1973.

American Council on Education. *Campus tensions: Analysis and recommendations.* Report of the Special Committee on Campus Tensions, S. M. Inowitz, Chairman. Washington, D.C.: Publication Division, 1970.

Aptheker, Betinna. *Higher education and the student rebellion in the United States, 1960–1969: A bibliography.* New York: American Institute for Marxist Studies, 1973.

Astin A. W., Astin, H. S., Bayer, A. E., & Bisconti, A. S. *The power of protest.* San Francisco: Jossey Bass Publishers, 1975.

# Bibliography

Bakke, E. W., & Bakke, M. S. *Campus challenge: Student activism in perspective.* Hamden, Ct.: Shoe String Press, Inc., 1971.

Bart, P., & Frankel, L. *The student sociologist's handbook.* Cambridge, Mass.: Shenkman Publishing Company, Inc., 1971.

Barzun, J. Tomorrow's university—Back to the middle ages? *Saturday Review,* November 15, 1969, LII (46), 23–25; 60–61.

Bayer, A. E., & Astin, A. W. Violence and disruption on the campus. *Educational Record,* Fall 1969, *50,* 337–350.

Bennis, W. G. *The leaning ivory tower.* San Francisco: Jossey Bass Publishers, 1973.

Berger, P. L. *Invitation to sociology.* Garden City, N.Y.: Anchor Books, 1963.

Berger, P. L. & Berger, B. *Sociology.* New York: Basic Books, Inc., 1972.

Berger, P. L. & Luckman, T. *The social construction of reality: A treatise on the sociology of knowledge.* Garden City, N.Y.: Anchor Books, 1967.

Berman, R. An unquiet quiet on campus. *New York Times Magazine,* February 10, 1974, pp.14–16.

Bloomberg, E.*Student violence.* Washington, D.C.: Public Affairs Press, 1970.

Boulding, E. Psychosocial design for non-violent change. Unpublished paper for the Round Table, American Orthopsychiatric Association, 48th Annual Meeting, Washington, D.C., March 21–24, 1971. (The model for secondary socialization was adopted from: *Socialization sequences and student attitudes towards non-violent social change.*)

Boyle, K. *The long walk at San Francisco State.* New York: Grove Press, Inc., 1970.

Braden, W. *The age of aquarius, technology and the cultural revolution.* New York: Pocket Books, 1971.

Brann, J. W. Campus turmoil continued at Columbia. *Commonweal,* October 4, 1968, *89,* 7–8.

Caplow, T. *Two against one: Coalitions in triads.* Englewood Cliffs, N.J.: Prentice Hall, 1968.

Carleton, W. G. Surrealism, revolution, reform—Or what? *VA Quarterly Review,* Autumn 1969, *45* (4), 563–578.

The Carnegie Commission Higher Education. *Dissent and disruption.* New York: McGraw Hill Book Company, 1971.

Cobban, Alan B., "Medieval Student Power," *Past and Present,* No. 53, Nov. 1971, pp. 28–66; Oxford: The Past and Present Society, 1911.

"Student Power in the Middle Ages," *Western Civilization,* Vol. I, William Hughes, Editor; Guilford; The Dushkin Publishing Group, Inc., 1985, p. 129.

Colleges denial of student rights cause most uprisings. *The Chronicle of Higher Education,* July 24, 1968, p. 1.

Coyne, J. R. *The kunquat statement.* New York: Cowles Book Company, 1970.

Curtis, J., & Petras, J. W. (Eds.). *The sociology of knowledge: A reader.* New York: Praeger Publishers, 1972.

Davies, P., & The Board of Church and Society of the United Methodist Church. *The truth about Kent State—A challenge to the American conscience.* 1973.

Douglas, J. D. (Ed.). *Understanding everyday life: Toward the reconstruction of sociological knowledge.* Chicago: Aldine Publishing Company, 1970.

Dunlop, R. *A bibliography of American studies of student political activism.* Eugene, Oregon: University of Oregon, Department of Sociology, 1969.

Ellsworth, F. L., & Burns, M. S. *Student activism in American higher education.* Washington, D.C.: American Personnel and Guidance Association, Student Personnel Series 10, 1970.

Epstein, C. *How to kill a college.* Los Angeles: Sherbourne Press, Inc., 1971.

Erlich, J., & Erlich, S. (Eds.). *Student power: Participation and revolution.* New York: Association Press, 1970.

Feuer, L. S. *The conflict of generations: The character and significance of student movements.* New York: Basic Books, 1969.

Flacks, R. Who protests: The social bases of the student movement. In J. Foster & D. Long (Eds.), *Protest! Student activism in America.* New York: William Morrow, 1970. Pp. 134–157.

Fleming, R. W. Reflections on higher education. *Daedalus—American education: Toward an uncertain future,* Vol. II, Winter 1975, *104*(1), 8–15.

Foleno, L. A. The school as a social system. Unpublished research paper for Education 310:520. Rutgers, Graduate School of Education, Spring 1968.

Foster, J. Student protest: What is known, what is said. In J. Foster & D. Long (Eds.), *Protest! Student activism in America.* New York: William Morrow, 1970. Pp. 27–58.

## Bibliography

Foster, J., & Long, D. (Eds.). An introduction to case studies. In *Protest! Student activism in America*. New York: William Morrow, 1970. Pp. 225–228.

Gerschenkron, A. The legacies of evil. *Daedalus—American education: Toward an uncertain future*, Vol. I, Fall 1974, *103* (4), 44–49.

Gordon, S. Missing an easy mark. (Review of Radicals in the university by E. E. Erickson, Jr.). *Change*, August 1976, *8*(7), 60–61.

Gurvitch, G. *The social frameworks of knowledge*. New York: Harper Torchbooks, Harper and Row, 1972.

Halleck, S. L. Hypotheses of student unrest. In A. Lightfoot (Ed.), *Inquiries into the social foundations of education*. Chicago: Rand McNally and Company, 1972. Pp. 89–103.

Hechinger, F. M. Dim view from Berkeley. *New York Times*, August 14, 1972, p. 27:1.

Heer, F. *Challenge of youth*. Translated from the German by Geoffrey Skelton. University of Alabama: University of Alabama Press, 1974.

Hersey, J. *Letter to the alumni*. New York: Bantam, 1970.

Hitch, C. J. *Some views on student attitudes*. Speech given as President, University of California, at Rotary Club Luncheon, Berkeley, April 2, 1969.

Hook, S. Can the universities survive equal access? (Review of *On the meaning of the university* by S. M. McCurrin). *Change*, September 1976, *8*(8), 59–61.

Horowitz, I. L. Scientific criticism and the sociology of knowledge. *Professing sociology: Studies in the life cycle of social science*. Chicago: Aldine Publishing Company, 1968.

Young radicals and professional critics. *Commonweal*, January 31, 1969, *90*, pp. 552–556.

Horowitz, I. L. & Friedland, W. H. *The knowledge factory: Student power and academic politics in America*. Carbondale: Southern Illinois University, 1972.

Hoult, T. F. *Dictionary of modern sociology*. Totowa: N.J.: Littlefield, Adams and Comany, 1974.

Jacobs, H. *The weathermen*. New York: Ramparts Press, Inc. 1970.

Kahn, E. J., Jr. *Harvard through change and through storm*. New York: W. W. Norton and Company, Inc., 1969.

Kahn, R. *The battle for Morningside Heights: Why students rebel.* New York: William Morrow and Company, Inc., 1970.

Karagueuzian, D. *Blow it up: The black student revolt at San Francisco State College and the emergence of Dr. Hayakawa.* Boston: Gambit, 1971.

Kelman, S. *Push comes to shove: The escalation of student protest.* Boston: Houghton Mifflin, 1970.

Keniston, K. *Radicals and militants: An annotated bibliography of empirical research on student unrest.* Lexington: Lexington Books, 1973.

*Youth and dissent: The rise of a new opposition, The unholy alliance* (with M. Learner). New York: Harcourt Brace Jovanovich, Inc., 1971.

Kerpelman, Larry C., *Activists and Nonactivists: A Psychological Study of American College Students;* New York: Behavioral Publications, Inc., 1972, pp. ix-x.

Kornstein, D., & Weissenberg, P. Social exchange theory and the university. In J. Foster & D. Long (Eds.) *Protest! Student activism in America.* New York: William Morrow, 1970. Pp. 447-456.

Krueger, M., & Silvert, F. *Dissent denied: The technocratic response to protest.* New York: Elsevier Scientific Publishing Company, Inc., 1975.

Kunen, J. S. *The strawberry statement—Notes of a college revolutionary.* New York: Avon, 1970.

Lane, R. E., & Sears, D. O. *Public opinion.* Englewood Cliffs, N.J.: Prentice Hall, Inc., 1964.

Letter, May 5, 1968. Excerpts from an unpublished letter written by a mother to her student-activist son who was involved in the student unrest at Columbia University, April 1968. The mother is a member of a college faculty in New Jersey.

Libert, R. *Radical and militant youth.* New York: Praeger Publications, 1971.

Lipset, S. M. *Rebellion in the university.* Boston: Little Brown and Company, 1971.

From apathy to revolt and back to apathy. (Review of *Student politics in America: A historical analysis* by P. Altbach). *Change,* Summer 1974, *6*(7), 56-57.

Lorenz, K. *Civilized man's eight deadly sins.* New York: Harcourt Brace Jovanovich, 1974.

Mannheim, K. *Ideology and utopia.* New York: Harvest Books, Harcourt Brace and World, 1952.

Mehnert, K. *Twilight of the young*. New York: Holt, Rinehart and Winston, 1976.

Merton, R. *Social theory and social structure*. New York: The Free Press, 1968.

Merton, T. *Conjectures of a guilty bystander*. Garden City, N.Y.: Doubleday and Company, Inc.,1966.

Michener, J. A. *Kent State, what happened and why*. New York: Fawcett Crest, 1971.

Nettler, G. A test for the sociology of knowledge. *American Sociological Review*, 1945, *10*, 393–398.

New York State Temporary Commission to Study the Causes of Campus Unrest. *The academy in turmoil, First report*. Albany, 1970.

101 campuses identified as demonstration scenes. *The Chronicle of Higher Education*, September 2, 1968, p. 5.

Orrick, W. H., Jr. Director of San Francisco State College Study Team. *Shut it down! A college in crisis, San Francisco State College, October 1968–April 1969*. A report to the National Commission on the Causes and Prevention of Violence. Washington, D.C.: Government Printing Office, June 1969.

Pareto, V. *The rise and fall of the elites: An application of theoretical sociology*. Totowa, N.J.: The Bedminster Press, 1968.

Parsons, T., & Platt, G. *The American university*. Cambridge, Mass.: Harvard University Press, 1973.

Peterson, R. E. The student left in higher education. *Daedalus*, Winter 1968, *97*(1), 293–317.

Peterson, R. E., & Bilorusky, J. A. *May 1970: The campus aftermath of Cambodia and Kent State*. Berkeley, Calif.: The Carnegie Commission of Higher Education, 1971.

Porter, J. N. *Student protest and the technocratic society: The case of ROTC*. Chicago: Adams Press, 1973.

President's Commission on Campus Unrest. *The report of the President's Commission on Campus Unrest*. Washington, D.C.: Government Printing Office, 1970.

Public Papers of the Presidents of the United States. Lyndon B. Johnson, Book 1, November 22, 1963 to June 30, 1964. D.C. U.S. Government Printing Office 1965. #11"Address Before a Joint Session of Congress November 27, 1963," pp. 8–10.

Remmling, G. W. *Road to suspicion: A study of modern mentality and the sociology of knowledge.* New York: Appleton-Century-Crofts, 1967.

Rosenkrantz, R. *Across the barricades.* Philadelphia: Lippincott, 1971.

Scott, J., & El-Assar. Multiversity, university size, university quality and student protest: An empirical study. *American Sociological Review,* October 1969, *24,* 702–709.

Scully, M. G. Who are/were those kids and why do/did they do those awful/wonderful things? *The Chronicle,* March 13, 1972.

Searle, J. R. *The campus war.* New York: The World Publishing Company, 1971.

Segal, P. *Annotated bibliography on student rebellion and revolutionary movements.* Claremont, Calif.: Claremont Graduate School, 1969.

Shibutani, T. Reference groups as perspectives. *American Journal of Sociology,* May 1955, *60,* 562–569.

Shimahara, N. K. American society, culture and socialization. In N. K. Shimahara & A. Scrupski (Eds.), *Social forces and schooling: An anthropological and sociological perspective.* New York: David Mckay Company, Inc., 1975.

Simon, K. A. & Grant, W. V. (Eds.). *Digest of educational statistics, 1968 edition.* Washington, D.C.: Government Printing Office, 1969.

*Digest of educational statistics, 1969 edition.* Washington, D.C.: Government Printing Office, 1970.

*Digest of educational statistics, 1970 edition.* Washington, D.C.: Government Printing Office, 1971.

*Digest of educational statistics, 1971 edition.* Washington, D.C.: Government Printing Office, 1972.

Sjoberg, G., & Nett, R. *A methodology for social research.* New York: Harper and Row, 1968.

Sloan, D. For the record: On the possibilities of newness. *Teachers College Record,* February 1978, *79,* 333.

Spady, W. G. The authority system of the school and student unrest: A theoretical exploration. *The seventy-third yearbook of the National Society for the Student of Education* (Uses of the sociology of education). Chicago: University of Chicago Press, 1974.

# Bibliography

Spiegel, J. P. *Campus disorders: A transactional approach.* Waltham, Mass.: Brandeis University, Lemberg Center for the Study of Violence, 1973.

Stanford, D. *Dylan Thomas.* New York: The Citadel Press, 1964.

Stark, W. *The sociology of knowledge.* London: Routledge and Kegan Paul, 1967.

Stevenson, W. J. *Radical political thought: SDS 1960–1968.* Unpublished doctoral dissertation, Rutgers University, 1972.

Stone, I. F. *The killings at Kent State, How murder went unpunished.* New York: A New York Review Book, 1971.

Taft, J. *May Day at Yale: A case study in student violence.* Boulder, Colo.: Westview Press, 1976.

Taylor, H. The student as teacher. In J. Whiteley (Ed.). *Students in the university of society.* Washington, D.C.: American Personnel and Guidance Association Student Personnel Series, 13, 1970.

Theodorson, G. A. & Theodorson, A. G. *Modern dictionary of sociology.* New York: Apollo Editions, 1969.

Toole, R. K. *An angry man talks up to youth.* New York: Award Books, 1970.

Trilling, D. On the steps of law library. In *We must march my darlings.* New York: Harcourt Brace Jovanovich, Inc. A Harvest/HBS Book, 1978.

Ulam, A. *The fall of the American university.* New York: The Library Press, 1972.

United States Congress, Senate. Permanent Subcommittee on Investigations of the Committee on Government Operations. *Staff study of campus riots and disorders—October 1967 –May 1969.* Washington, D.C.: Government Printing Office, 1969.

*U.S. News and World Report.* Student violence: Into a more dangerous era. May 18, 1970, 68(20), 28–31.

Urban Research Corporation. *Student protests 1969: Summary.* Chicago:1970.

Wallerstein, Immanuel, "The University Crisis: The Transitional and The Chronic," *Student in the University and in Society,* John Whitely, ed.; D.C.: American Personnel and Guidance Association, 1970.

*University in turmoil,the politics of change.* New York: Antheneum, 1969.

Wallerstein, I., & Starr, P. *The university crisis reader,* Vols. 1 and 2. New York: Vintage Books, 1971.

Whiteley, J. W. (Ed.). *Students in the university and in society.* Washington, D.C.: American Personnel and Guidance Association, Student Personnel Series 13, 1970.

Wolff, K. H. (Ed.). *From Karl Manheim.* New York: Oxford University Press, 1971.

Wood, J. L. *Political consciousness and student activism.* Sage professional papers in American politics, Vol. 2, Series No. 04–015. Beverly Hills and London: Sage Publications, 1974.

Wrong, D. H. Reviews. *Change,* April 1972, *4*(3), 66–69.

Zorza, R. *The right to say we: The adventures of a young Englishman at Harvard in the youth movement.* New York: Praeger Publishers, 1970.